The American Writer

ALSO BY LAWRENCE R. SAMUEL
AND FROM MCFARLAND

New York City 1964: A Cultural History (2014)

The American Writer
*Literary Life
in the United States
from the 1920s to the Present*

LAWRENCE R. SAMUEL

McFarland & Company, Inc., Publishers
Jefferson, North Carolina

ISBN (print) 978-1-4766-7102-4
ISBN (ebook) 978-1-4766-2992-6

LIBRARY OF CONGRESS CATALOGUING DATA ARE AVAILABLE

BRITISH LIBRARY CATALOGUING DATA ARE AVAILABLE

© 2018 Lawrence R. Samuel. All rights reserved

No part of this book may be reproduced or transmitted in any form or by any means, electronic or mechanical, including photocopying or recording, or by any information storage and retrieval system, without permission in writing from the publisher.

Front cover image © 2018 iStock

Printed in the United States of America

McFarland & Company, Inc., Publishers
Box 611, Jefferson, North Carolina 28640
www.mcfarlandpub.com

Table of Contents

Preface   1

Introduction   4

Chapter 1 • The Modernists, 1920–1939   11

Chapter 2 • The Realists, 1940–1959   37

Chapter 3 • The Intellectuals, 1960–1979   65

Chapter 4 • The Individualists, 1980–1999   93

Chapter 5 • The Nomads, 2000–   120

Chapter Notes   149

Bibliography   159

Index   161

Preface

As with many American writers, it all began innocently enough. Some twenty years ago, an editor for a scholarly press asked me if I would be interested in having my dissertation turned into a book. "Sure, why not?" I reckoned, especially with the $500 advance I was offered. Little did I know that seeing and holding the finished product a year or so later would spark a deep, unabated desire over the next two decades to be published. Already having a job of sorts, I had no intentions of being a part-time writer much less a full-time author, but some strange force pushed me to scribble down words whenever I had the chance. Books that did not exist, but that I believed should, had to be written, and, if no one else was going to do it, it had to be me. I quickly deduced that writing two clean pages a day, day in and day out, would give me a manuscript in six months, making consistency at least as important as inspiration. My scribblings soon evolved into a mission; having no kids at the time, leaving a robust body of work after I was gone would be my legacy, i.e., a literal paper trail that would ensure a kind of immortality.

Twenty books later, I felt the need to put my personal literary experience into some context by knowing more about the careers and lives of American writers who came before me. It quickly became apparent while doing research that I was hardly the only person to suffer from the writing bug and thus I was further spurred to diagnose the causes of this virulent condition. Being a cultural historian by trade, I felt that examining the role of writers within American society over the past century seemed to make the most sense in terms of approach. Such an exercise would not only help other writers come to terms with their own creative impulses, but add to their understanding of literary culture in this country—something useful in itself. Besides all that, writing about writing seemed like a fun thing to do and a way, perhaps, to improve my own craft.

The irony that no book fully dedicated to exploring literary life in the United States over the course of the last century has been published has not been overlooked. As our primary storytellers, writers deserve a full telling of their own story—one that goes beyond the more encyclopedic, anthological literary histories usually found on reference bookshelves. The book argues that those who have used language as their creative medium have held a unique and special place in our collective imagination, making the writer a fascinating character in the real-life American narrative. Part of my goal here is to show that taking on the responsibility to either document the past, present, or future of society or to create stories that reveal who we are as a people has been a weighty one. This proposition is intended to give writers the long overdue credit they deserve.

Still, this work shows that the American writer—actual or imaginary, famous or not-at-all famous—has often been situated on the margins of society as an outsider looking in. More observers than participants, writers are typically peripheral to the main action, i.e., they are the narrator of a story rather than the protagonist. While there is some romance and glamour attached to the profession, writers have also been commonly depicted as tortured souls or as hacks barely scraping by (consider Joe Gillis, William Holden's character, in the 1950 film *Sunset Blvd.*). Pecking away in an attempt (usually, a vain one) to produce the Great American Novel or its cinematic equivalent (think *Barton Fink*) is another literary or cinematic cliché that is grounded in considerable truth. Print journalists, meanwhile, have frequently been assigned the role in uncovering the truth in some sort of cover-up or conspiracy, again casting the writer as a kind of lone wolf working against the system. From Nick Carraway to the millions of bloggers today, writers are generally perceived as intellectual artists documenting an aspect of the human condition—a representation that warrants fuller exploration.

Although this book focuses on writers, it is of course impossible to ignore the work they produced. *The American Writer* locates individuals within the creative climate in which they operated, making the

Preface

work also, at some level, a history of American literature and the publishing business since the 1920s. Agents, editors, and readers—each obviously playing an important role in the careers and lives of writers—are thus also main characters in the story. I try not to make much of a distinction between "high" and "low" forms of writing, seeing both serious literature and popular entertainment as essential pieces of the story. And while the social divisions of race, gender, and class have obviously been important factors and are addressed in the book, I devote more attention to the American writing community at large versus "hyphenated" writers, e.g., gay, Jewish, black, or female. The most compelling stories are those that illustrate what we have in common and those to which we all can relate.

The American Writer begins with the end of World War I and continues to the present day. Literary life in the United States entered an entirely new orbit in the 1920s that, in many ways, endures to this day—hence those chronological boundaries. Regarding sources, the spine of the book relies on contemporary trade and popular magazines and newspapers, as well as scholarly references. Hundreds of different sources—many of them forgotten—draw from journalists' writing of "the first draft of history." Professional writers penned much of the source material themselves, lending a direct, first-hand account of the story. Books and journal articles are used to frame the story, provide valuable context, and locate the work within mainstream scholarship. Literary life has of course played a recurring role in books, movies, and television and these too serve as prime fodder for the work. Typically overshadowed by his or her work, the American writer is brought into the light, something that is in itself a worthy pursuit.

Introduction

> *"American writers, at least those of us who are fortunate enough to support ourselves in the field, are by and large a lucky lot."*
> —Bryan Burrough

American writers like Burrough are indeed a lucky lot. Making a decent living by putting words down on paper is a rare privilege, and one that millions of people have tried to achieve. For at least the past century, Americans of every stripe have devoted much of their lives to becoming professional writers. Why this is so? What makes writing such a compelling dream for so many people to chase? By investigating literary life in the United States over the last hundred years or so, we begin to answer this and many other questions related to the peculiar art of writing, while also increasing our understanding of the role of creativity in American culture.

Given the widely acknowledged capriciousness of writers, which has considerable basis in fact, it should not be surprising to learn that literary life in this country has been an unpredictable affair with some of the plot-zigzagging of a dime novel. This work shows that the cultural trajectory of the American writer has taken many twists and turns. Five broad archetypes have defined the American writer since the 1920s, illustrating the fact that while much of an individual's literary life has remained relatively constant over the past one hundred years, powerful social, economic, and technological forces have greatly impacted the climate in which authors have operated. A new and different kind of American writer emerged shortly after World War I as the surge of modernity recast the arts and artists themselves, making this the logical place to begin the book. "A new school of more interesting writers is forming," Brand Whitlock observed in 1923, thinking it to be "a vigorous school, free, enthusiastic, with all the mettlesome qualities of youth."[1] Modernists rejected virtually everything that came before them, and were determined to forge a brand of literature that both reflected and shaped the progressive, daring ethos of the times.

While the Depression hit writers hard (as nonessentials, books and magazines relied on discretionary income), those able to influence public opinion through words were recognized and rewarded during World War II. This positive wartime experience laid the fountain for the postwar years, when writers sought out and found economic stability—a rare feat for any artist. The countercultural years were turbulent ones for all Americans, of course, but, with all varieties of intelligence valued, writers received an unprecedented level of respect. Although the American writing community fragmented towards the end of the twentieth century, creativity escalated as a form of social currency, ensuring that artists of all kinds were deemed as one strain of the cultural elite. Recently, the digital revolution has radically transformed all aspects of the literary universe, shifting the balance of power in the publisher/author relationship and affording the American writer an unprecedented level of direct access to the marketplace.

While a broad survey of literary life in the United States has been lacking, many fine books about American writers have of course been published. Ben Tarnoff's *The Bohemians: Mark Twain and the San Francisco Writers Who Reinvented American Literature*, for example, traced the story of Twain and other "bohemian" Western writers in the late nineteenth century who, the author argued, played a key role in shaping modern America. "The Bohemians would bring a fresh spirit to American writing," Tarnoff posited, while in the process breaking up the monopoly that Eastern writers and publishers had held.[2] Harold Bloom's *The Daemon Knows: Literary Greatness and the American Sublime* took the interesting approach of pairing great American writers' works "in conversation with one another," a conceit that vividly revealed why literature truly matters.[3] And in his *Moral Agents: Eight Twentieth-Century American Writers*, Edward Mendeson took a deep dive into the work of eight major American writers who, in the author's words, not just practiced their craft but "seized for themselves the power and authority to shape American literary culture."[4]

Introduction

American literary histories geared toward an academic audience also have contributed much to the field. Richard Gray's *A History of American Literature*, *The Norton Anthology of American Literature* (edited by Nina Baym) and the *New Literary History of America* (edited by Greil Marcus and Werner Sollors) are each excellent surveys that help locate American literature within the nation's history.[5] "Microhistories" of our literary landscape are also valuable towards piecing together the puzzle of the American writer. From Alfred Kazin's *God and the American Writer* to *At the Fights: American Writers on Boxing* (edited by George Kimball and John Schulian), such histories shed much light on particular aspects of literary life in this country.[6]

Rather than focus on certain authors, take a sweeping view of American literature, or concentrate on a particular topic or genre, *The American Writer* attempts to illustrate the meaning of being a writer in this country. Various themes naturally emerge while tracing the lives of these artists (primarily authors, particularly novelists, but, to a lesser extent, journalists, screenwriters, playwrights, and others). Certainly intriguing has been the compulsion that has driven otherwise perfectly sensible people like myself to want to be writers. The process is typically frustrating and the financial rewards paltry (the average income of writers hovers around the poverty line), yet wave after wave of young adults have flocked to the field to earn the privilege of calling themselves writers or authors. A current promotional piece for Gotham Writers, a Manhattan school for writing, reads, "Everyone has a story, especially you"—an explanation as good as any to justify this continual literary mania.

The urge for humans to tell stories one way or another is indeed a primal one, ensuring there will always be people who wish to be writers despite all good reasons not to be. In fact, too many Americans have decided they will be writers, thinking they will beat the odds by finding some measure of success, even if fame and fortune are not in the cards. There has been an oversupply of writers in this country (and probably most others) for decades, which contributes to the not-very-attractive economics of the business.

As in any arena, however, Americans have tended to focus on those writers who were able to rise to the top of their chosen profession. Much interest has thus been expressed in the "stars" of the field, i.e.,

Introduction

those writers who were considered the best or most commercially successful. Famous personalities do indeed make appearances in the book, but I am more interested in the role that all writers have played within American culture and, especially, their creative process. Writers' politics—more often than not considered liberal or "radical"—are also frequently referenced, as is their loyalty to the country. Regionalism is woven into the subject, with American writers often viewed as a product of their environment, i.e., the South or West, state, or city. Writers have had a special relationship with New York City, of course, making Gotham the literary capital of the world for much of the past century.

One running theme revolves around the making of money or, in many writers' cases, the lack of it. Except for a lucky few at any given time, writers appear to have been continually financially strapped, victims of the relatively low monetary value that has been set for their work. While writing is a creative art, it is also a business, with a decent living at the center of professionals' concerns. There has thus been a consistent tension between doing what one loves to do (or at least what one is good at) and being fairly compensated for it—more so than in other occupations. The feast or famine nature of writing has served as one of the defining elements of the business; dreams of hitting it big were common, as was the knocking out of words for modest fees or meager advances in order to pay one's bills. Naturally, some times were better than others for writers, economically speaking. Financial rewards for writers generally correlated with their social status, which often wavered in the public's eye.

Another key theme is the persistent question of whether there has been an authentic and original American literature. Especially early in the century, many wondered if those in creative professions in this country, including writing, were producing world-class work. "There are some captious people who claim that we have no real literature," Thomas L. Masson observed in 1919.[7] Europe had a much longer and richer literary history, making American writers compete, to some extent, with those across the pond (both dead and alive). Like other art forms in this country, notably music and painting, American literature (and writers themselves) has suffered from what can be described as an insecurity complex. American writers have been cast in the long shadow of Europe, making them appear as literary upstarts who are constantly trying to find a unique voice or vocabulary. Was there a unique American style of writing? critics both here and abroad asked, and, if so, what was it? Interestingly, these doubts about the legitimacy of American fiction have fed into the alleged emotionally frail (or, conversely, volatile) character of writers, putting psychology at the center of the story.

To that point, American writers' offbeat personality profiles (brainy but neurotic, observant but hypercritical, etc.) have made them largely enigmatic, misunderstood figures. Stringing words together is, after all, almost always a solitary exercise, locating writers in a non– and sometimes anti–social role. "To my landlady and her female lodgers on the second and third floors I believe I am a man of mystery, if not an object of actual suspicion," a writer living in a New York boarding house remarked in 1919, this "because I remain in my room with my typewriter while other men are slamming the door and running for the subway at 8:15."[8] Not too much has changed over the last century, with some of this outside-the-mainstream image self-perpetuated. In his 1978 *The American Jeremiad*, Sacvan Bercovitch wrote, "American writers have tended to see themselves as outcasts and isolates," with many authors assuming the role of "prophets crying in the wilderness."[9]

Not surprisingly, then, writers have often been perceived and portrayed as quirky, eccentric, and occasionally belligerent, a reputation that is arguably well deserved. The fact that writers have operated behind the scenes has helped to create a kind of enigmatic aura around them, both collectively and individually, that is not unlike the one surrounding other artists. This has been both an asset and a liability to writers, making them appear somehow special and gifted, yet also difficult and temperamental. A good number of American writers were famously jealous and hostile towards their peers. Robert Frost was not shy about his contempt for other poets such as Wallace Stevens, for example, and novelist Mary McCarthy and the playwright Lillian Hellman shared an incendiary, long-running feud. Truman Capote and Gore Vidal were longtime adversaries, while novelist Tom Wolfe referred to John Irving, John Updike, and Norman Mailer as "the Three Stooges" of American literature.[10]

Popular culture has reinforced the unconventional, even peculiar image of the American writer. In movies, TV shows, and even novels,

Introduction

it is not unusual to see writers as disheveled, destitute, and/or drunk (something interesting in itself as it was likely a writer who created the character). In films such as *Manhattan* (1979), *The Shining* (1980), *The World According to Garp* (1982), *Deathtrap* (1982), *The Player* (1992), *Deconstructing Harry* (1997), *Fear and Loathing in Las Vegas* (1998), *Finding Forrester* (2000), *Wonder Boys* (2000), *The Royal Tenenbaums* (2001), *Adaptation* (2002), *American Splendor* (2003), *Sideways* (2004), *Capote* (2005), and *The Squid and the Whale* (2005), writers are morally dubious, socially challenged, or downright psychically impaired characters, tempting viewers to think negatively of those who occupy the profession in real life.

While the Jessica Fletcher televisual character in *Murder She Wrote* was laudable (if overly prim and proper), the Hank Moody role in *Californication* was more typical of how pop culture has treated the American writer. Suffering from emotional issues and writer's block (not to mention an addiction to various vices), Moody, played by David Duchovny, is an unequivocal train wreck, although by the end of the series in 2014 he has righted his course. Some of America's best novelists including Saul Bellow, John Updike, Philip Roth, and Kurt Vonnegut have often used writers as their protagonists, and not in a particularly flattering way. Middle-aged men (like the authors themselves), whose best days are definitely behind them, populate these novels; their struggle to find meaning and purpose in their lives can be seen as emblematic of the existential angst commonly believed to be a defining quality of the American writer.

Again, stereotypes relating to American writers have some basis in fact. Alcohol (and alcoholism) has been a defining feature of literary life in this country, with research showing a clear link between writing and drinking that may be neurologically based.[11] In her 2014 *The Trip to Echo Spring*, Olivia Laing examined the role that alcoholism played in the lives of six American writers (John Berryman, Raymond Carver, John Cheever, F. Scott Fitzgerald, Ernest Hemingway, and Tennessee Williams), finding deep, psychological connections between their respective addictions and creative genius.[12] Some writers were even under the influence while they worked. Edna St. Vincent Millay wrote her 1921 *Vanity Fair* essays while sipping gin, William Faulker's 1936 *Road to Glory* was whiskey infused, Carson McCullers penned her 1940

Introduction

The Heart is a Lonely Hunter with copious amounts of hot tea and sherry, Raymond Chandler relied heavily on gimlets (and vitamin shots) to produce his 1946 *The Blue Dahlia*, and Capote gulped down double martinis when working on his 1965 *In Cold Blood*. The Beats, meanwhile, preferred drugs to alcohol, and created some of their best material while using Benzedrine, heroin, and psychedelics.[13]

Other themes also become apparent through looking at the history of the American writer. After the modernists redefined the American novel in the 1920s, fiction was continually criticized—almost always seen as in a state of decline (despite the publication of some great work). "Current American literature seems to me richer in minor figures than ever before, but poorer in major figures than it was in Emerson's day," noted Henry Hazlitt in 1932. This was a typical commentary on the state of fiction at that time.[14] The Great American Novel—a work of fiction that is acknowledged as revealing key insights into our national character at a particular time—seemed to be always dying, already dead, or purely a myth. "Why all the craze over the great American novel?" asked an editor for *The Bookman* in 1927, of the mind that it was simply "a mirage that keeps the weary novelist and reader always on the go."[15] As well, each generation of writers rejected the body of work created by the previous one, a very American idea and practice. Finally, while literary styles, genres, and theories were continually in a state of flux, and the technological tools writers used always evolving, the same questions were being asked. What makes a writer? How is he or she different from other people? Where do his or her ideas come from? Why would anyone want to write a book? The mystery of the creative process is the backstory of the American writer, making this work at some level an exploration of the human condition.

Chapter 1

The Modernists, 1920–1939

> *"He writes so easily and so cleverly, he constructs so swiftly and so surely, and the result of his abounding energy is often so entertaining as to make one feel that in the past too much time must have been wasted in producing dull masterpieces."*
> —Thomas L. Masson, speaking of young American writers in 1920

In May 1928, the editor of *Forum*, one of the elite highbrow magazines of the day, took note of the recent transformation of American literature. "All who read are aware that something has happened to the novel," the editor wrote, pointing out that the kind of fiction being produced by one of the leaders of this new movement, Theodore Dreiser, was vastly different than anything written by nineteenth-century British authors like Charles Dickens or William Thackeray. "The essence of this change is the rise of a new and purposeless attitude toward life," the editor proposed, this rather dark and gloomy perspective "sometimes called modernism."[1]

Importantly, it was American novelists who were redefining literature in the 1920s and, in the process, what it meant to be a writer. Between the world wars, the landscape of the American writer shifted dramatically, as modernism in all its forms seeped into literature and the other arts. The American writer came into his and her own over the course of these two decades, as a new kind of literature steeped in modernity came into being. It was the "passing of a literary era," as one journalist noted in 1925, as the musty, verbose style of writer popular before World War I became seen as thoroughly antiquated. A new breed of literary stars including Sinclair Lewis, F. Scott Fitzgerald, Ernest Hemingway, John Dos Passos, Sherwood Anderson, John Steinbeck, William Faulkner, Henry Miller, Eugene O'Neill, and Pearl Buck appeared on the scene, with their rather brash brand of fiction often labeled "American realism" (and sometimes "lusty literature"). Quite simply, nobody had ever read anything quite like what the modernists were creating; the history of the written word had been irrevocably altered.

Not coincidentally, these writers were very much part of what came to be called the "lost generation," that group of young adults who came of age during the war, and had yet to fully recover from the trauma of that terrible event. (Indeed, the phrase became popular after Hemingway used it in an epigraph in his 1926 *The Sun Also Rises*.) With the market crash of 1929 and slide into the Great Depression, however, the flurry of excitement surrounding the new wave of modernist literature abruptly ceased. While the cream of the crop, such as the members of the Algonquin Round Table, lived it up at fabulous cocktail parties in New York City, the majority of writers in the country were simply trying to pay the rent by churning out 50 cent "juveniles" and other pulp fiction. Beyond the economic challenges, American writers became a much-maligned group, their unpleasant personalities matched only by their oversized egos. The American writer took a wild rollercoaster ride between the wars, one that was entirely consistent with the unpredictable nature of the profession.

A Peculiarly Impudent Youth

The elevated status of the American writer could be detected immediately after World War I. One clear sign was the publication of a much-anticipated, three-volume work on the rise and progress of American literature by Cambridge University Press. It is difficult now to appreciate how significant the official canonization of American literature by an elite English publisher was at the time. The late nineteenth century work of New England "Fireside" poets like Henry Wadsworth Longfellow and James Russell Lowell was undoubtedly beautiful, but many critics had justifiably felt it was not distinctly Amer-

Chapter 1 • The Modernists, 1920–1939

ican.[2] Much skepticism still surrounded the New World's contribution to not just American literature but to all of the humanities, in fact, making Cambridge's history of the best verse and prose of the nineteenth and early twentieth century a blessing of sorts of the arts in the United States. "It surveys the whole higher life of an entire community," noted *The Living Age* in its 1920 review, thinking that the greatest American writers of the past and present had finally received the respect and legitimacy they deserved.[3]

Greater recognition of America's literary canon was certainly exciting, but the appearance of a different kind of fiction in this country was nothing less than thrilling to some (and rather appalling to others). Those steeped in the Victorian tradition found the supposed realism in some novels being published in the early 1920s startling, especially those in which the main story took place in smaller towns or cities. Sinclair Lewis's 1920 *Main Street* arguably received the most attention of this new brand of fiction, and became seen as emblematic of what was termed the "revolt from the village" in American literature. Novels that revealed "the revolt from the village" by American writers displayed a "critical attitude toward everything as opposed to the complacent, the optimistic, the sentimental," Louis Wann suggested in the *Overland Monthly* in 1925.[4] Some critics accused *Main Street* as lacking credibility and being more atmospheric and superficial than having good, progressive storytelling.[5] Others, however, argued that this was precisely the point. Noted critic Henry Seidel Canby felt that the new school of American fiction was important if not always artistic, and it was the symbolic value of books like *Main Street* that made them great works of literature.[6]

Although there was general agreement that contemporary American fiction by younger writers deviated from all previous literature, it was difficult even for experts in the field to say exactly how. This generation of novelists was no doubt gifted but had yet to reach its full development, making it premature to offer a complete assessment of their work. After Scribner published his first two novels (*This Side of Paradise* in 1920 and *The Beautiful and the Damned* two years later), F. Scott Fitzgerald emerged as a kind of figurehead for group. In his 1922 *Contemporary American Novelists, 1900–1920* Carl Van Doren considered Fitzgerald to be "the most promising of our very young writers," believing that he would eventually enter "the front ranks of our novelists." Fitzgerald was "brilliant, bitter, sometimes chaotic but always young with a peculiarly impudent youth," Van Doren continued, thinking that the author's refusal to cater to "public consumption" ironically accounted for his meteoric rise.[7]

When Van Doren used the term "public consumption," he might have well said female readers. Although there was no hard research, there was little doubt that women far outnumbered men as readers of fiction in the early 1920s. In a 1921 article for *The Yale Review*, Joseph Hergesheimer asserted that ten thousand women read a novel to one man, obviously an exaggeration but one he used to make a point. Women represented a "feminine nuisance in American literature," he felt, as writers keen on having a bestseller catered to their supposedly trashy tastes when it came to fiction. Women were making significant strides along gender lines at the time, of course, but that fact seemed to have been lost on Hergesheimer. The popular novelist not only held that women had no interest in substantive literature but that professional men were too tired to read novels after a hard day at the office, each a highly questionable claim. Some well-read women understandably reacted angrily to Hergesheimer's accusation, making it clear that they were an asset to, rather than "nuisance in," American literature.[8]

Almost everyone at the time would have agreed that the finest verse and prose did indeed represent the "higher life" of a particular society. If anthropology was the science of man, "fiction at its best is the study of man," argued Gertrude Atherton in *The Bookman* in 1922, thinking that excellent novelists, short story writers, and dramatists were able to capture the soul of humanity. Atherton, a popular novelist herself, felt that members of the younger school of American authors such as Lewis and Dos Passos had yet to realize this level of skill, however, thinking they had not worked off their bitterness towards the war and their distaste of the optimistic fiction of Victorian days. (The former's *Main Street* had been published but great works like *Babbitt*, *Elmer Gantry*, and *Dodsworth* were still to come, and the latter's outstanding *U.S.A.* trilogy was a decade away.)[9]

Whether or not the modernists were still works in progress, thousands of American writers had dreams of becoming the next Sinclair

Chapter 1 • The Modernists, 1920–1939

Lewis or John Dos Passos as literature became a more lucrative career in the 1920s. Not just money but fame would be quickly realized with a bestseller, both amateur and professional writers believed as they pecked away on their Remingtons, Underwoods, or Coronas. The reality was, however, that fame (and often money) was fleeting even for those writers who were skilled and lucky enough to land on a bestseller list. (*The Bookman* published the first such list, with the *New York Times* list not appearing until 1931.) Not unlike magazines and newspapers, novels had become a disposable product in the new mass consumption society, lending their authors a brief moment in the sun until the next celebrated book came along. First-time authors who had success found it difficult to match with their second effort as readers turned their attention to new writers. Am I just repeating myself? many authors asked themselves as sales continued to drop with each new book. Other authors wondered if their writing skills had surpassed the tastes of the general public, little compensation for now being considered on the literary B-list.[10]

One anonymous writer detailed the less than glorious life he had realized after having a bestseller on the first go-round. Describing the experience as "the agonies of literary success," the writer of nonfiction made it clear that he was now doing quite well in the field, relatively speaking, but that the ride had been full of ups and downs. Having made it as a working writer wasn't "nearly as jolly as I had been led to suppose," the author admitted in 1928, as nothing could compare to the initial exhilaration that came with sudden fame. After a couple months of being in the spotlight, "the ego comes home to roost," as the giddiness of celebrity morphs into an everyday, workmanlike existence of simply doing what has to be done. Royalties on the book did not nearly cover his family's expenses, making him trapped in a sort of purgatory of keeping the machine he had built running.[11]

Yet another initially successful writer told his better-be-careful-what-you-wish-for story. As he attested, it was not unusual for fiction writers like he who were working on a novel to sadly learn that their story comes to a rather sudden halt. Voila! A short story was born, as any writer (or other artist) knows that wasting good material is anathema (and financially unwise). Novels and short stories were seen as distinct literary expressions, but that did not stop writers who had once been in the limelight from turning the beginning of the former into the latter. Assuming the glory days would continue, writers were known to build an addition to their home or enroll their kids in private school, decisions that were regrettable when the gravy train slowed down. Signing contracts for well-paid magazine serials was often the next step, "whereupon mediocrity sets in," according to this writer. Working with illustrators (magazine stories of the time typically included drawings) was no fun it all, and publishers often wanted the same kind of material if the writer's first submission had proved popular. "He has said all he had to say in the first thirty eight stories, but money talks," this writer explained, now in an endless loop of having to repeat himself to satisfy the public. "God help successful authors," he concluded, not at all what young writers wanted to hear as they imagined themselves as the toast of the literary town.[12]

Tousled-headed, Unkempt, Underbred and Ill-natured

As Woody Allen so nicely captured in his 2011 film *Midnight in Paris*, the rush of modernism in the 1920s in both the United States and Europe made some nostalgic for a literary and artistic past that was no more. Amazingly enough, some octogenarians and nonagenarians in New York City could recall the literary circle that used to gather in Pfaff's cellar saloon at the corner of Bleecker Street and Broadway in the 1850s and 1860s. (Until recently, one could still have a beer there.) That circle, of which Walt Whitman was famously part, served as the true beginnings of bohemian New York, making it a seminal part of the city's literary history. (Women were occasionally invited to the group's festivities.) While newspapermen of the day had a steady income, the writers of the group relied on selling a piece to magazines like *Harper's* or *The Atlantic* in order to make ends meet. Like writers of future generations, members of the Pfaff circle could somehow afford copious amounts of beer and tobacco but not the rent for an apartment of their own. Two events—the outbreak of the Civil War and, almost as significant in literary terms, the relocation of some of the best of the city's writers to Boston—spelled the end of the fondly remembered

Chapter 1 • The Modernists, 1920–1939

Pfaff circle. In the late nineteenth century, another generation of writers consisting of staff members of the weekly *Puck* magazine would meet at a beer hall on Houston Street, but this too seemed like ancient history in the Roaring Twenties.[13]

Boston was unarguably the literary center of the United States after the Civil War, with that title passing to New York by the end of the nineteenth century. By 1920, however, Chicago was home to many of the best American writers, leading (Baltimore resident) H. L. Mencken to declare it the literary capital of the nation. Mencken, the leading literary critic of the day, believed Chicago to be "the most thoroughly American of American cities," borrowing on Carl Sandburg's already famous poem about the city (first published in 1914). Sandburg, Dreiser, Sherwood Anderson, Booth Tarkington, Frank Norris, Ben Hecht, and many other writers called Chicago home, and there was both a new poetry movement and little theater movement percolating in the city. Bookstores were popping up on nearly every street corner of the city, and every Saturday at noon the local literati gathered at a big round table at Schlogl's, a German restaurant (the Midwestern equivalent perhaps to the daily lunching of the "Vicious Circle" at the Algonquin Hotel).[14] New York was affected, Boston senile, and Philadelphia stupid, the outspoken Mencken felt, while Chicago was vital and energetic, making it the ideal place for American writers looking for inspiration.[15]

Given the yearning to identify an authentic American literary form in the 1920s, Chicago did indeed appear to be the right place at the right time. "We are so busy finding truly representative authors, authors who express the essence, the distillation, of America," wrote Kenneth Burke in 1923, like Mencken believing that Chicago was the most likely city to make that discovery. Sandburg had aptly captured the town's working class dynamism, something that Burke felt was the foundation for great writing. "To be unmistakably American, a work of art must hitch up its trousers, shake frail gentlemen's hands with vigor, and wipe the stain of tobacco juice from its lips before speaking," Burke put it rather poetically. Making a clear break from Europe demanded strength, confidence, and boldness, and the big cities of the Northeast were too much like the Old World to achieve that. As much as Burke praised Chicago, it too would eventually lose its artistic potency, he envisaged, predicting that our pioneer spirit would next be found out west, specifically San Francisco.[16]

According to one local expert, however, San Francisco was nowhere nearly ready to inherit the throne of literary capital of the United States. San Francisco had been rebuilt in the twenty years since the 1906 earthquake flattened the city, but its literary climate remained decidedly rough-and-tumble. "We [the Bay Area] are at the beginning of a new era in letters," wrote Mrs. Frederick H. Colburn, in the *Overland Monthly* in 1927, seeing, "no great outstanding personalities on our literary horizon." Instead, San Francisco and Oakland were filled with "tousled-headed, unkempt, underbred and ill-natured" writers, according to Colburn, adding coarseness, vulgarity, eccentricity, and egoism to the list of their undesirable attributes. (One has to only imagine what Colburn would have thought of the Beats and hippies that populated the area a few decades later.)[17]

Although it had a thriving literary scene, the Corn Belt had a different problem. Many novels by writers from Wisconsin, Kansas, Minnesota, Illinois, Nebraska, Iowa, and the Dakotas were being published, but they seemed preoccupied with a single theme. "The secret yearnings and complexes of the average farmer's wife" had somehow taken hold in midwestern fiction, so much so that it had virtually become a genre unto its own. "Almost every unsuccessful newspaper reporter and small-time college instructor seems to be writing 'elemental' stories about the strong, silent, bovinely stupid women of the Great Open Spaces Where Men Are Morons," Weare Holbrook of *Forum* put it in 1924, thinking "a stupendous monotony has been achieved." The city had typically been the locale for wickedness in American fiction, but now it appeared to be the country where children were born out of wedlock and jealous husbands held their wandering wives captive.[18]

The South was very much a part of the modernist movement of the twenties. "A casual glance at the recent literary output of the United States discloses immediately the fact that the South has suddenly burst into colorful bloom," Hershel Brickell wrote in 1927, making the case that writers below the Mason-Dixon line were, for the moment at least, "the center of literary interest in this country." It was unclear why Southern writers had made such a rapid ascent, especially when there was no recognizable school that bound them together in any discernible

Chapter 1 • The Modernists, 1920–1939

way. Young writers from the South were eagerly submitting material to journals such as *The Reviewer, The Southwest Review,* and *The Sewanee Review* in hopes of jumpstarting their literary careers.[19] Much attention was beginning to be paid to Mississippian William Faulkner after the publication of his *Soldier's Pay* and *Mosquitos*. South Carolinian Edwin DuBose Heyward's *Porgy* was considered a landmark book at the time for its sympathetic portrayal of African Americans. (His wife Dorothy soon adapted the novel into a Broadway play, after which it evolved into the 1935 opera *Porgy and Bess* with music by George Gershwin.) Many argued that James Branch Cabell of Richmond, Virginia, was actually the best American writer of the day. Dozens of other Southern writers were doing great work, however, challenging Mencken's famous remark that the South was a literary desert.[20]

The Drift of the Current

As critics noted at the time, modernists were geographically dispersed but they were almost all young. More so than ever before, there was a generational divide between American writers in the 1920s, a reflection of the recent ascendance of youth culture. Older, more established writers tended to copy the style and method of their British counterparts, making them essentially "echoes" of a non-native literary form. Even some of the greatest American writers used what could be described as an "artificial" process, it was argued, drawing on the British literary canon as a source of inspiration.[21] Edith Wharton and Booth Tarkington may have been the country's most accomplished novelists and Robert Frost the most renowned poet, but each represented a literary style that was out of sync with where literature was headed.[22]

As important, both average writers and a good many literary stars in this country did not seem distinctly American, a quality that had gained cultural currency across the arts. Their work was perfectly acceptable and usually sold well, but all the talk in the literary trade was about the brash young writers and their audacious, sometimes salacious novels. "The writers who belong to the modern movement as a conscious school are fewer in number, but more clamorous for notice," Paul Elmer More observed in *Forum* in 1928, noting the group's deliberate attempt to create a new kind of fiction that had as little connection as possible to Europe. Modernists believed that rejecting or ideally destroying the past would lead to liberation from the Old World's political, religious, and social repression that had been brought to New England by the Puritans. From this perspective, Lewis, Dos Passos, Dreiser, Anderson and a few other American writers of the 1920s could be legitimately called cultural revolutionaries, using their respective gifts to spark social change.[23]

Not everyone, of course, was enamored by the kind of fiction that had caused such a stir since the end of the war. For some, a novel becoming a bestseller (often because of serialization in a popular magazine) was reason enough not to read it. How could it be so good if the masses liked it? more snobbish readers asked fellow readers innocently recommending a popular book. "I don't care for modern fiction," might be another reply, followed by the claim that "I read only the classics." Interestingly, it was more often young intellectuals who dismissed modern fiction as a fad equivalent to the latest dance craze like the Charleston. Even book reviewers who praised a novel when it was published were known to change their tune when it hit the bestseller list, treating its success among the general public as a strike against it.[24]

Whether purposely or not, modernists used science as a model to create what Sherlock Bronson Gass called "the sensation of life" in their novels. Taking an objective approach would lessen personal bias, the writers believed, making what they produced more authentic than the stylized fiction of the nineteenth century. On a grander level, modernists believed, science offered an attractive alternative to the religious dogma that had weighed humans down for centuries, the latter functioning as a kind of yoke on individual potential. Stream of consciousness—one of various links between modern literature and psychoanalysis—was one of the techniques being used by writers trying to see things as they were without the filter of socialization. Like scientists, modern novelists were to attempting to understand the universe as it was, each profession dedicated to solving the mystery of life.[25]

Others weighed in on what Robert Herrick called "the drift of the current" of the American literary scene. One of the more notable things about the new fiction was that, even though first-time authors were

Chapter 1 • The Modernists, 1920–1939

often writing the books, major houses were publishing them, and offering big advances. Herrick believed that each novel by itself was not especially noteworthy but, when the movement was viewed collectively, the body of work did indeed represent something significant. Every generation of artists tended to produce a crop of work that consciously or unconsciously blazed new territory, however, leading some to wonder if this literary movement was truly different from those of the past. Herrick, a novelist, believed it was, with younger American writers "reflecting something actually felt and observed in the life about them"; this was the thing that made them and their work genuinely distinctive. "What is going on is a kind of sociological survey of the United States in the guise of fiction," he astutely observed, the between-the-world-wars glorification of scientific thinking clearly impacting the arts.[26]

One notable person, however, was not at all impressed with the current vogue of American novelists to approach their craft like it was a social science. The landscape of fiction had grown tiresome by 1926, F. Scott Fitzgerald believed, as authors embarked on what he described as a "literary gold rush." Just as Herrick maintained, many writers were basing their novels on the kind of sociological research that Robert and Helen Lynd were using to produce their landmark study *Middletown: A Study in Modern American Culture*. Some were heading to farms to gather material, others to the mountains, and still others to the Caribbean, with the findings then set within a novelistic framework. "The literary beginnings of what was to have been a golden age is as dead as if it had never been written," Fitzgerald put forth, too many authors (seventy or eighty, he estimated) trying their hand at the "modern novel" diluting the original, bold idea. Fitzgerald had good things to say about E.E. Cummings's 1922 *The Enormous Room*, however, as well as the first work of a writer named Ernest Hemingway. Hemingway's *In Our Time*, a collection of fourteen short (and long) stories, was the most exciting thing to happen to American literature since Joseph Conrad's 1900 *Lord Jim*, he felt, quite an accolade from arguably the most celebrated writer of the day.[27]

If there was a single word to describe the new wave of fiction being published, both good and bad, it very well might have "pessimistic." Even before the war, more astute critics observed that the optimism

Americans were famous for had faded somewhat, a general sentiment that could be detected in the literature of the times. A certain kind of anxiety or gloominess could be found in the works of Emerson, Whitman, Twain, Henry David Thoreau, and Edgar Allan Poe, and only intensified after the 1918 flu epidemic and devastating war. "If we believe her writers," Regis Michaud wrote in *The Living Age* in 1926, "America is not happy." The protagonists of novels by Lewis, Dreiser, Anderson, Hecht, Willa Cather, and Zona Gale were all constrained by forces that were beyond them; their realistic tales were much about suffering, oppression, and a lack of control over one's own destiny.[28] While both critics and readers generally adored Hemingway's *The Sun Also Rises*, which was published that same year, they were taken aback by that novel's cynical streak (and how much of the time the cast of characters were drunk). It was no coincidence that the title of the book came from Ecclesiastes, the Old Testament book filled with less than cheerful utterances such as "everything is meaningless." "Mr. Hemingway uses it [the title] to connote that general futility which exudes from the tale he tells and the life he depicts," noted Charles W. Ferguson, considering the author (who was currently living in France) to be one of the "five rising stars in American fiction."[29]

It was difficult to dispute the idea that psychology was playing a role in the negative outlook towards life being expressed in novels such as *The Sun Also Rises*. As the technique of stream of consciousness suggested, many detected a good dose of psychoanalysis in modern literature, with writers possibly venting their frustrations in order to be liberated from them. ("Freudianism" was of course all the rage in urban America in the 1920s.) The economic boom the nation was experiencing may have been affording material comforts but not psychic freedom, one might conclude after reading recent fiction, with American writers tapping into this zeitgeist of despondency.[30] Some critics, however, were less than impressed with the streak of pessimism that was running through contemporary novels. "We are producing in the United States quantities of fiction in which not only is there no illumination, but there is a disposition to insist on a general state of muddled unsatisfactoriness as the American norm," wrote Mary Austin, finding all the despair in modern novels more distracting than anything else.[31]

Megalomania in Varying Degrees

After the stock market crash of 1929, one did not have to look to modern novels to find doom and gloom. Like most businesses, publishing was hit hard by the Depression, marking the end of what had been a renaissance for American writers. More people appeared to be borrowing books from other readers versus buying them for themselves, for one thing, not a good thing for publishers or authors. Booksellers too were hurt by a reduction in sales, with a considerable number closing up shop in the early 1930s. A clear sign of the times was the shuttering of the leading literary journal, *The Bookman*, in 1933. Still, books were not going to go away completely, with many readers viewing them as an escapist form of entertainment much like movies. There also seemed to be no slow down in the number of people who wanted to be writers. In fact, many of the newly unemployed now had time to explore their literary side, making the 1930s a fertile period for the American writer despite the economic crisis.

There was no single path in the making of an American writer, of course, but there were some common developmental life experiences that many people choosing to write for a living shared. At some point in one's youth, a leaning towards introversion could often be detected, after which future fiction writers were known to embellish stories when recounting them to friends and family. Teachers and parents might then encourage the imaginative teenagers to write such stories down with pen and paper or a typewriter, partly as a learning technique and partly to channel the fantasies in a different direction. Those with genuine promise as an author were apt to construct brief passages of prose, many of which were filled with the kind of angst and deep philosophical thoughts that only teens possessed. Parents would frequently share these proto-short stories with a select group of neighbors who had an appreciation for quality literature, with rave reviews almost certainly guaranteed.[32]

It was at this point that writers-in-training were ready to make the big leap to publication. Local newspapers were often the selected target, although school publications and fraternal magazines were other good choices to get one's name in print. After a few such small but important successes, the budding writer was off to college, where he or she joined literary groups of like-minded wordsmiths. Classes in literature and philosophy provided ample reading for students to shape their worldview that would likely later inform their own work. Upon graduation, the writer joined thousands of others wanting to make a career out of it, often keeping a day job (advertising was a popular choice) while constantly creating material on the sly in hopes a literary agent or editor would find some of it marketable as a magazine article or book.[33]

It is unclear how this quite pleasant, logical process produced the monsters published American writers were now often said to be. The excitement surrounding the rise of the modernists of the 1920s had worn thin after the crash, with a backlash of sorts directed at anyone and everyone who wrote for a living. Only recently viewed as exalted guides to and interpreters of life with special insight into the human condition, authors were experiencing a precipitous fall from grace as they became commonly seen as imposters. "Authors are as a tribe an ungrateful, egotistical, selfish and unprincipled lot," claimed an anonymous publisher in 1931, finding them to be a general nuisance to everyone, especially their poor families who had to live with the pests. Besides being jealous of any other author's success, they were usually, contrary to popular belief, dull company and "surprisingly stupid." Poor sales of a particular book was never the author's fault; rather, it was the publisher's or, perhaps, the public's, specifically the latter's preference for "shockers" (what would today be called thrillers) over great literature. It was not unusual for authors to call the publisher to tell him or her that the little bookshop on the corner had no copies of their respective book on the shelf. Booksellers too were used to authors coming into their store and complaining about where their book was displayed (something that more often than not would result in an even more hidden location for the volume).[34]

Were authors truly that awful? Some argued that they were more victims than anything else, and did not deserve the condemnation they were as a group receiving. Spending their days alone in a room, authors were relatively harmless people, defenders pointed out, the act of writing hardly a cruel or violent one like that of criminals. As well, authors instantly became the subject of criticism once their work was published, making them the target of anyone with any opinion. Critics were

Chapter 1 • The Modernists, 1920–1939

also not reluctant to comment on authors' private affairs, and, without any factual support, suggest reasons why they constructed the stories they did. Magazine editors were not above hiring one writer to attack the work of a known rival, something that often resulted in a literary cockfight. If anything, it was the publishing business that was the problem, those with a broader vision pointed out, its competitiveness turning the once congenial literary climate into a battlefield where authors were cast as villains and pitted against each other.[35]

Others continued to chime in on the less attractive characteristics of writers, however. One anonymous literary agent felt compelled to say that he knew a few authors who did not think of themselves as geniuses and believed their books were genuine masterpieces, but they were more the exception than the rule. "The rest, an overwhelming majority, exhibit megalomania in varying degrees," the agent explained in 1935, their arrogance either a natural trait or acquired as a writer. Authors were a necessary evil, according to some agents, exactly what a good many of the former thought of the latter. Authors were on good behavior when in the presence of editors and publishers, fully aware which side of their bread was buttered. But, when with those who represented their work, authors' much uglier side came out, making agenting a tougher job than it appeared. Why do I get such small advances? Why are my books not reviewed (or getting poor reviews)? Why isn't the publisher advertising my book, and why are the covers so bad? Agents had to routinely field such questions from most of their clients, making the profession as much ego rehabilitation as literary representation.[36]

Authors' reputation had gotten so bad by the early 1930s that one observer felt compelled to (humorously) question whether they were really people. "Are authors human beings?" J.B. Priestley asked in 1931, answering his own question with a single word: hardly. Priestley, a well-known British writer, was not precisely sure when authors (including himself) failed to be human beings, thinking the process occurred gradually, maybe over a period of a decade or so. "When you consider the envy, the jealousy, the peevish vanity, the monstrous conceit, the wild antics of authors," he wrote in 1931, "you can hardly ask yourself, 'Are these creatures men and women?'" Only publishers of classics were happy people, Priestley maintained, as that was because all their authors were dead. Priestley had a theory about why authors were so horrible: they were more observers of ordinary life than participants in it, making them feel superhuman or even godlike. Life was simply raw material for an author, this perspective accounting for their self-absorption and antisocial behavior.[37]

A Peculiar Tribe

Priestley's theory was a good one, but it could simply have been the demands made on successful authors that turned them into ogres. Famous writers were far more accessible than they are today, with readers not reluctant to contact them by mail, phone, or even by showing up at their office or home. (Even well known authors were likely to be listed in the local telephone book.) A popular author might receive hundreds of invitations from women's clubs to teas, and just as many requests to judge writing contests or lend his or her name to a charity or cause. Authors routinely received lengthy letters by the bag load from people offering a critique of one of their works, many of them wishing to establish a regular correspondence about all things literary. (A fair number came from convicts with considerable time on their hands.) Religious zealots formed a contingent of letter writers all their own, warning of a wrathful God should the authors continue to have his or her characters pursue their wicked ways. Another group consisted of people with stories to sell, with yet another asking for money because of some alleged misfortune.[38]

There seemed to be no end to what might be called "literary parasites" wanting one thing or another from an author of some acclaim. Autograph hounds aggressively sought signed copies of books, sometimes only to sell them at auctions for their greater value. Local literary societies were a particular thorn in authors' sides, sometimes asking for a personal appearance, other times requesting detailed personal information for an upcoming book talk. Even worse, English teachers in public schools had recently taken to telling students learning about a particular writer or book to send letters to recognized authors to ask their opinion on the subject.[39] Not surprisingly, there was no shortage of letters from young people wanting advice on how to become a successful writer, as well as large packages containing manuscripts for the author to not only critique but to make grammar and spelling corrections. One might conclude from all this that authors' time was considered to be in the public domain, more so than in any other profession. Was it any wonder that authors developed a surly streak towards the public?[40]

The case against American writers went from the sublime to the ridiculous in the early 1930s. Because of authors' widely acknowledged difficult personalities, those considering marrying one should think twice before heading to the altar, one observer of the literary scene recommended. "Is it rash to marry an author?" asked Osbert Burdett in 1932, coming to the conclusion that it very well might be. More so than others, authors were generally perceived as "nervous" people, this (over)sensitivity directly related to their preoccupation with critical observation. In a nutshell, he argued, authors were not easy folks to live with, making co-habitation an arrangement that was fraught with peril. "He is a prism, analyzing, sifting and codifying everything that comes, even unconsciously, within the focus of his refractivity," Burdett wrote, this almost machine-like way of thinking part and parcel of his choosing such a "queer occupation." (Women authors were a whole other matter, according to Burdett.) Even if officially a bachelor, authors were already married to their Muse, he maintained, making a relationship with a mortal woman seem trivial compared to the one they had with a goddess. If there was any good news to women in love with an author, it was that he was likely to be more interesting, sympathetic, and understanding than an average Joe, these positive traits also coming with the literary territory.[41]

In such an anti-literary climate, "queerness" was considered a fitting way to not just to describe the profession but writers themselves. Freud and other notable psychoanalysts had posed interesting theories regarding how creative geniuses of all sorts were made, making the psychological probing of famous literary figures past and present a popular sport. Maladjustments in childhood were viewed as a key contributing factor for artistic genius, and early physical disabilities believed to lead to intellectual "compensations" such as writing. Great minds were the product of an almost supernatural bequeathing, according to prevailing thought, an idea that those in creative professions typically did not try to dispute as it lent a certain mystery to their profession. Likewise, traumatic experiences and hardships such as poverty and undernourishment were commonly seen as ideal prerequisites for high achievement in literature and other arts, making it not surprising that a label of "queerness" was assigned to both writers and writing.[42]

Even some writers freely admitted that those of a literary persuasion were odd ducks. "Let us admit that we are a peculiar tribe," I.A.R. Wylie wrote in *Harper's Monthly*, the secret that this was true having only been recently being revealed. Indeed, the idea that someone was perfectly capable of writing thousands of words (sometimes hundreds of thousands) about a character that didn't exist could be considered at least a bit strange. Wylie believed the "outing" of writers took place in the United States around 1927 when, because of the luxury to do so, more scrutiny was paid to everything. American writers, long existing in relative obscurity, were suddenly popular figures, raising the expectations of the reading public. The realization that a large percentage of writers were not particularly intelligent was nothing less than shocking; the ability to describe people, places, and things in vivid detail apparently did not translate to anything else. People in other professions could do something else if they had to, but apparently the only thing writers could do is write. Not only were writers not the smartest people in the room but they were unfunny, poor conversationalists, and, as a rule, physically ugly, many agreed, making their removal from anonymity an unfortunate decision.[43]

Whether or not they really were churlish boors who had wisely chosen a profession where they could be in a room all by themselves for long periods of time, writers seemed to fall into one of two different camps. Some truly wanted to write whether they got published or not, while others simply wanted to be writers for whatever social status they believed it afforded. Many authors who had had some success were convinced they were now famous, a false assumption given the fact that many Americans did not read books. (Even Sherwood Anderson, one of the most well known authors in the country, was occasionally mistaken for the playwrights Maxwell Anderson and Robert Sherwood.)[44]

Authors' misperception of fame was in part due to overzealous readers (or, in many cases, non-readers) wanting to make a good impression. Strangers routinely claimed they "loved" an author's book upon meeting him or her, a complete lie since they had not even read it. Ladies hosting literary nights or dinner parties with an author at their home were known to rush out and buy a copy of the esteemed guest's latest book and display it prominently. (The newness of the book was a giveaway that the pages had never been turned, however.) Authors' most dreaded question—"What are you working on?"—was frequently asked at such uncomfortable-but-sometimes-necessary events. Authors not unusually constructed an answer even more fictional than their fiction (Anderson would say a history of the American Civil War because it sounded impressive), either not wanting to reveal the actual subject of their next book or, just as likely, having absolutely nothing in the works.[45]

A Set-up and a Cinch

Authors as a group may or may not have been a species unto their own, but it could not be disputed that they had a nearly infinite array of working styles. (Booth Tarkington famously wrote in a bathrobe.) For whatever reasons, the public was unusually interested in how, when, and where writers did their job, significantly more so than those in other occupations. (How long it took to write a book was a particular source of fascination.) The image of the nervous writer at the flat-topped desk with student lamp tapping away at a rickety typewriter in the wee hours of the morning surrounded by piles of discarded manuscript pages as well as a dictionary, thesaurus, and pot of black coffee and/or cheap gin was a popular one but mostly apocryphal. Novelists were likely to work in a relaxed rather than frenetic manner, allowing their characters to generally dictate the action and chart their own destinies after the author gained a solid understanding of the kind of people they were meant to be. Many eschewed an outline or synopsis, feeling such a thing would limit the characters' possibilities and make the writing stilted. Some writers who could afford it dictated their stories to their secretary, an approach that sped up the process considerably. Mornings were generally the most productive hours, with afternoons set aside for revisions or the business side of the profession. A dozen rounds of revisions was not unusual, making the process more one of rewriting than writing. A good number of between-the-wars authors still used a pen or pencil to produce their material, thinking that a typewriter put one on autopilot and made one's work seem generic (something that would be said with the advent of the personal computer a half century later).[46]

Because writers could presumably work anyplace, where they decided to set up shop was deemed newsworthy. Rich and famous authors typically moved about the world according to season and based on where their social set happened to be in a concerted effort to find a proper balance between work and leisure. Another group found country life to be the ideal setting for writing, with the peace and quiet to be had amidst nature just the thing to attract their muse. For many if not most recognized American writers, however, there was no place like New York City to call home in the 1930s. "In New York there is the endless challenge to work," wrote George Jean Nathan in 1936, "a constant current of electrical energy that penetrates into even the most quiet and secluded writing room, an invisible but clearly felt flying flag to lead the spirit on." Writers like Nathan had tried to work near the sea and in the mountains but felt the natural beauty was too distracting, ironically finding a certain composure and tranquility within metropolitan life. Other contemporary writers apparently agreed; Dreiser, Wharton, Cather, Fitzgerald, and Dos Passos all had produced some of their best work in New York. As well, the leading publishers, top agents, and elite "little magazines" were based in the city, making Gotham the best place for writers to sell their work and be part of a thriving literary community.[47]

If the stereotype of the wild-eyed author madly trying to meet a publisher's deadline was off the mark, so was the expectation of what one would be like in person. Readers tended to believe they already knew authors based on their writing, and were often surprised to learn that he or she was someone quite different in the flesh. A novelist who stretched the boundaries of the imagination could be, if one didn't know better, a lawyer or accountant after having the chance to meet him or her. Those attending a dinner where an author was asked to speak were frequently shocked that this person who wrote so well was

Chapter 1 • The Modernists, 1920–1939

far less equipped verbally. (It is positively painful to watch Joseph Cotton's character, a popular writer of western pulps, try to make an impromptu speech when asked to do so in the film *The Third Man*.) Readers were much more likely to be disappointed after meeting a literary idol or hearing him or her speak, finding that rather pedestrian person not nearly as impressive as the power of their written words.[48]

It can be understood why so many people wanted to be writers despite their many alleged flaws. Besides the urge to follow one's muse, there was the simple fact that there were few other occupations in which one could make money purely by documenting one's thoughts. No real training, trade, skill, or college degree was necessary to write, and one didn't have to join a union or "know somebody" to find work. In simple business terms, writing was, assuming one could create a product that could be sold, an unbeatable proposition. "I hit upon the great secret that if you can create goods, wares and merchandise with no cost for raw materials, overhead, labor, advertising, or selling, you are almost practically certain to make a profit," explained Clarence Budington Kelland in the *Saturday Evening Post* in 1933. Kelland liked people to think producing literature was hard work, but he knew otherwise. "Making money with a brain like mine is a set-up and a cinch," Kelland confessed, wary of being lured away by a steady stream of "can't lose" business opportunities that came his way but never panned out.[49]

Unfortunately, too many people in the United States believed they had such a brain. Publishers were continually bombarded with manuscripts from writers convinced that they could and should be authors. Manuscripts arrived by mail in every form—rolled, loose, bound, wrapped in newspaper—and in all containers imaginable, including stationary boxes, cake boxes, shoeboxes, metal tins, briefcases, portfolios, and even suitcases and trunks. Some were written in pencil, others in pen. Typed manuscripts could be single-, double-, or triple-spaced. Others had been self-printed to give the appearance of a book. The color of paper might be white, yellow, brown, green, or any number of other shades in an attempt to stand out from the crowd. Some manuscripts were illustrated, and others bound in vellum, parchment, or leather. Ribbons and tassels were surprisingly common, as was the inclusion of a photograph of the author. Some submissions included letters of recommendation from a minister, others high school report cards (and still others offers of gifts, money, and sex). The opportunity to come into the office to read the work aloud would be much appreciated, some writers felt compelled to mention. Once in a while a manuscript would arrive that included photographs of the author's family and friends in character in order to illustrate the story, this worthy enough to make the rounds of a publishing house. "The trouble is that everybody in America is sure he can write," observed a publisher's reader responsible for screening manuscripts, blaming teachers for encouraging too many students to try to become the next Thornton Wilder or Edna Ferber.[50]

While the packaging of manuscripts was often nothing short of remarkable, it was the text where this reader was taken aback by the writing ability of the average person attempting to become an author. About a quarter of the fiction submitted defied the boundaries of space and time, he reckoned, with Mars and Utopia among the most common themes. Interplanetary travel and the future each allowed aspiring authors to stretch the limits of the imagination, after all, exactly what they believed publishers wanted to see. Remaking the topography of Earth to suit one's story was not unusual (were there really that many caves on Long Island?), and metaphors came by the bulk, even in a single sentence. The writers themselves were also an endless source of fascination for this sympathetic reader, the latter finding the former to be well intended but delusional about their level of talent. Old maids really did pen novels of lusty passion, mild-mannered bookkeepers stories of wild adventure, and tough thugs tender tales of love for their pooch, he reported, concluding that, "the worse they write, the nicer they are."[51]

A Furious International Competition

For all the aspiring authors doing whatever they could to get published, there were many more people who wished they could write a book but had no idea how. In addition to curiosity about the sheer mechanics of it all, i.e., the how, when, and where of writing, non-writers were apt to wonder where a novelist's story came from and whether or not it was "true." No one asked an artist whether his or painting was "true," meaning based on real life, yet this was considered a legitimate question for men and women of letters. Likewise, many readers assumed novelists attempted to make their stories as true to life as possible, forgetting perhaps that fiction was a plastic art, just as much as painting or sculpture. One almost had to be a writer to understand the magic that took place when things were clicking; deadlines, financial considerations, and what others (editors, readers, and critics) might think all disappeared in the presence of one's muse, a process that could not be easily explained.[52]

Given that imagination was an unlimited resource for a creative mind, it was an interesting fact that relatively few novelists were able to sustain a successful career over a long period of time. "All of us have been puzzled by the violent ups and downs of literary reputations," Desmond MacCarthy noted in *The Living Age*, he like many surprised by "how authors rise in favor, and how quickly, often, admiration of them declines."[53] A glance at the bestseller lists from the past decade or so indeed revealed that there were many "one-hit" or perhaps "two-hit" wonders, and only a handful of authors who consistently produced widely read books. Did most authors have just one or two good books in them, one had to wonder, with nothing really original to say after that? Or was it that publishers were keen on promoting the next *wunderkind* to satisfy the demands of a public always wanting something new and different from last year's model? No one really knew. Social and cultural forces were no doubt at work in making the modernist authors of the 1920s seem quite out of place in the more sober 1930s. The rebellious, mostly autobiographic novels of the previous decade had lost much of their appeal, as communitarian interests took precedence over those of the individual.[54]

Economics were also playing a large role in the emergence of a less ebullient period for the American writer in the 1930s. Unemployment was at record highs during the Depression years, and writers likely suffered as much as any other profession except perhaps bankers and others in the world of finance. Because authors did not hold "real" jobs, however, they were essentially immune to being laid off or let go like those who worked nine-to-five. (Journalists were another matter.) "A writer can never be out of work because there is no work for writers to do," a 1936 editorial in the *Saturday Review of Literature* noted,

The American Writer

another good example of the peculiarity of the field. The fact was, however, that only a small minority of published authors actually wrote for a living; most supported themselves with teaching or other jobs, or were fortunate enough to be funded by a foundation or wealthy patron who was passionate about literature (or the writer himself or herself—a well-kept secret within the business). More so than other occupations, Darwinism seemed to define writing in the United States, with the fittest, i.e., most marketable, authors likely to survive and the vast majority forced to pursue other ventures.[55]

The Depression had certainly made it more difficult for American writers to pursue their careers, but it was greater competition that perhaps posed the greater long-term challenge. For one thing, living writers had to contend with dead ones, the number of the latter always increasing. It was the shrinking of the world after World War I, however, that made all writers vie for a limited number of readers and book contracts. More intense global competition had affected almost all American industries by the early 1930s, with publishing no exception. Serious readers could choose from not just numerous American writers but contemporaries from Great Britain (e.g., George Bernard Shaw, H.G. Wells, Rudyard Kipling, James Joyce, Aldous Huxley, Virginia Woolf, Bertrand Russell), France (e.g., Paul Valery), Germany (e.g., Thomas Mann), Austria (e.g., Sigmund Freud and Carl Jung), Russia (e.g., Maxim Gorki), and more from Italy, Spain, Norway, and other countries. "From now on," noted American journalist Henry Hazlitt, "the American writer must struggle desperately for survival against a furious international competition."[56]

The biggest potential windfall for writers was when Hollywood called. The 1930s were a golden age for the movies, of course, with novels used as a prime source to develop screenplays for films. The money to be made by selling a novel to a movie studio was huge by publishing standards, something that no doubt influenced the way that fiction writers created their material. A call from a publisher that Hollywood was interested in buying the rights to one's book had become the dream of many American writers, even more so than seeing one's name on the bestseller list. Margaret Mitchell's *Gone With the Wind* had been a huge hit in 1936 and into 1937, but the news that it would be made into a movie by David O. Selznick and star Clark Gable and

Chapter 1 • The Modernists, 1920–1939

Vivien Leigh made many writers think their novel might be just the stuff for the big screen. An initial meeting might be set up with an author, an editor or publisher, and a producer or two, often at the fanciest restaurant in town.

Things often did not go as smoothly as writers thought they would during and after the wining and dining, however. Those in the picture business tended to be quite brusquer than usually cordial amiable editors, for one thing, and it was surprising that the producers had likely not actually read the book. (Readers in the studio's scenario department, usually women, typically developed a one-page digest of a short story or book that producers used to evaluate possible film projects.) Producers, used to being pitched verbally, preferred that novelists tell them the plot in person, and in remarkable brevity. It quickly became clear that filmmakers viewed all material formulaically, and that they were primarily interested in which particular slot the novel in question fit. Authors were also not pleased to learn that movie people often optioned their book only because another studio was considering doing so or was planning to make a similar film. And more often than not, the whole thing eventually fizzled out, as story analysts and boards deemed to be experts in public taste determined that the "vehicle" would not be turned into a "property." "The peak of interest was passed, days grew into weeks, the telephone calls thinned," one novelist explained after his brush with Hollywood, sad to learn that his project had been "shelved."[57]

Not as much money usually came with receiving a Pulitzer Prize in fiction, but such an accolade was considered the most prestigious achievement in publishing since the award was established in 1918. The terms of the award was that the prize went to "a distinguished novel, preferably dealing with American life," but after that it was a matter of taste among the judges. At least as much attention was paid to who did not receive the prize as who did. Ellen Glasgow was a notable omission, for example, having not won the prize despite having written no less than five first-rate novels between 1925 and 1935. Dreiser, Fitzgerald, Hemingway, Dos Passos, and Steinbeck had not won the prize by 1938, while Tarkington (*The Magnificent Ambersons*, *Alice Adams*), Wharton (*The Age of Innocence*), Lewis (*Arrowsmith*), Cather (*One of Ours*), and Mitchell (*Gone With the Wind*) had. Prize committees were known for choosing dark horses, such as Margaret Ayer Barnes (*Years of Grace*), Louis Bromfield (*Early Autumn*), Oliver LaFarge (*Laughing Boy*), T.S. Stribling (*The Store*), Margaret Wilson (*The Able McLaughlins*), Caroline Miller (*Lamb in his Bosom*), and H.L. Davis (*Honey in the Horn*). Only time would determine the true merits of a novel, all agreed, with some winners almost instantly forgotten and others destined to be classics.[58]

As the country began to pull out of the Depression in the late 1930s as it prepared for possible war, things began to look up for the American writer. A long view in fact revealed that contemporary writers were in a much better place than those of generations past. "The writer's social position, whatever his economic status may be, has vastly improved since the days when even the most gifted had to go through life with their hats in their hands," Train wrote in the *Saturday Review of Literature* in 1938. Marketers had again begun advertising in magazines, good news for article writers and novelists hoping that some material from their recent book would be serialized. "Slick" magazines like the *Saturday Evening Post* paid well, and were thus the most reliable source of income for a full-time writer.[59]

Best of all, the revival of the American writer appeared to be national in scope, with new, distinct literary schools being formed across the country. Santa Fe had a school of writers who worked alongside notable visual artists like Georgia O'Keefe and Alfred Steiglitz in the mid–1930s, while nearly every state in the Midwest including Minnesota, Missouri, Iowa, and Michigan was said to have a particular writing style. California was a writer's universe all its own, particularly given the abundant work to be had scribbling dialogue and scenes for the movies now that the industry shifted west. As well, radio scriptwriters had recently become a hot commodity as broadcasters looked for content to fill airtime, another potential revenue stream if one had an interesting story with commercial appeal.[60] Another era loomed for those determined to spend much of their lives putting words on paper, one that would turn out to be very fruitful for the American writer.

Chapter 2

The Realists, 1940–1959

> *"American novelists play the role of keepers of the social conscience."*
> —Max Lerner, *America as a Civilization* (1957)

Anyone lucky enough to be seated at the Stork Club in 1940 might have been surprised by who was likely to be seated at the next table. On any given night that year, the "writing crowd," as it was commonly called, accounted for more than half the tables at the unofficial headquarters of "café society." Beautiful debutantes and their millionaire escorts waited not so patiently to be seated, wondering where all these rather odd-looking, not very rich folks came from. The same thing could be found at the other "smartest" places in town such as Voisin's, Jack and Charlie's, the Passy, the Colony, El Morocco, the Plaza's Persian Room, the Iridium Room at the St. Regis, and the Monte Carlo. The city's finest eating places, such as Delmonico's, were also filled to the gills with writers, editors, and publishers. "Look behind a Scotch grouse steaming on a platter in the most expensive New York restaurant and you will find a literary face," noted St. Clair McKelway in *Harper's Magazine*, amazed to find the aristocracy "fight[ing] for caviar elbow-to-elbow" with people who trafficked in words to make their living.[1]

The reversal of fortune for the American writer, in a wholly positive sense, was clearly evident. Considered strange if not inferior human beings through most of the 1930s, their intelligence and character very much in question, writers had by 1940 become seen as part of the cultural elite. Much of this turnaround had to do with the erosion of their generally leftist, anti-business politics; most writers were now part of the emerging "consensus" that would guide the nation though the next war and postwar years. "They are as firmly entrenched in government and society circles as the Morgans and Astors used to be," McKelway wrote, as a select group of writers mixed and mingled with the rich and powerful in both New York and Washington, D.C. Dozens of members of the literary set, including Claire Boothe, Bennett Cerf, Edna Ferber, Moss Hart, Lillian Hellman, Ernest Hemingway, Henry Luce, Dorothy Parker, Louella Parsons, Damon Runyon, William Saroyan, Walter Winchell, and Alexander Woollcott, were not just eating fancy foul in New York but had become visible presences on the smart set's "circuit," i.e., Saratoga in August, Palm Beach in January, and opening nights at any event that mattered throughout the year. Most impressively, the elevation of writers and literature was a national phenomenon, as a new kind of prestige was attached to the written word.[2]

The renaissance of the American writer would not, however, last long. With the country's entry in World War II at the end of 1941, lavishness of all kinds was discouraged, and writers were figuratively or literally enlisted in the battle to save democracy. Many writers would come out of the war with a great first book, e.g., Herman Wouk's *The Caine Mutiny* or James Jones's *From Here to Eternity*, but the collective body of work that followed was widely criticized for lacking the vigor that the modernists had so embodied in the 1920s and 1930s. Postwar American writers were, perhaps more than anything else, "realists," interested in weaving the social turmoil of the times into their stories. Another label thrust upon these writers was "the anxious generation," that term reflecting the group's alleged insecurities and fears, including those related to expressing the limits of their imagination because of the social forces that were in play at the time. Fittingly, perhaps, a new group of American writers would challenge their older colleagues (and almost everyone and everything else) in the late 1950s, foreshadowing the artistic and cultural revolution that was about to come.

The American Way of Life

The popularity of some writers was so great in 1940 that their success caused unintended problems. Authors of bestsellers continued

Chapter 2 • The Realists, 1940–1959

to be barraged by fan mail, phone calls, and unannounced visits to their homes, so much so that every so often one felt the need to plead readers to stop. In an "open letter to the reading public," one anonymous author told "bankers, Rotarians, librarians, teachers, parents, pupils, church groups, and club members everywhere" why she could not respond personally to each of them. It would be one thing if readers' messages were just to register an opinion, she explained, but this was rarely the case. Instead, some sort of request was typically included, this the thing that was most frustrating. If readers really liked authors' work, they would let them just write rather than have them spend their valuable time corresponding with all the people who wanted to have them lecture, answer detailed questions about their personal lives, explain the themes of their books, donate to a charity, join some organization, or invest in a can't-miss business opportunity.[3]

A more pleasant indication of the favorable times for authors was their great demand in Hollywood. More novelists and playwrights were heading west to translate their own material to the screen, write scripts based on the work of others, or develop original stories. As always, big money was the draw, but, as the saying went, there was no free lunch. "Authors" suddenly became "writers" when working on a movie, a demotion of sorts given the creative limitations that were placed on the latter. A good number of famous authors had flopped spectacularly in Hollywood after having their wings of imagination clipped by directors and studio executives wanting the plot to go in a different direction or the characters to speak different words. (Ben Hecht, who wrote the screenplays for *The Front Page, Scarface, Gunga Din,* and *Wuthering Heights,* was a rare exception.) Sometimes a perceived change in the "public's taste" would create the need for a complete rewrite after a script was finished, making many an author wonder why he or she decided to take the job in the first place. But many authors could not resist the temptation to try their hand at the pictures; the fat paychecks and glamour of Tinseltown were just too alluring to turn down despite the reality of no longer being in full creative control.[4]

Some better-known authors were themselves flirting with the more visible side of show business in the early 1940s. Alexander Woollcott was appearing in a stage production of *The Man Who Came to Dinner* in 1941, for example, while Sinclair Lewis was playing a role in

Shadow and Substance. Casting oneself in a play that one had written had become a thing to do among more thespian-inclined writers. Robert Benchley co-starred in his short feature film *How to Behave*, Christopher Morley was both directing and acting in his revival of *The Trojan Horse*, and Thornton Wilder was playing the stage manager in a production of his hit *Our Town* (which had won a Pulitzer Prize and had already been made into a movie). Noel Coward, Edna Ferber, J.P. Marquand, and Charles Hanson Towne were other writers stepping out into the footlights. While not very common, these men and women were following a long tradition of writers who occasionally performed in public. Shakespeare had done so early in his career, and Moliere's acting abilities were said to equal those of his literary skills, not too bad company in which to keep.[5]

The emergence of a more powerful kind of literary agent had much to do with the higher public profile and greater social status of American writers and their work in the early forties. Literary agents were rare in the nineteenth century, with the few (usually older women) practicing the trade acting not much more than deliverers of manuscripts to publishers. But by 1940 the agent had become a central force in the world of publishing, earning his or her 10 percent of the take by demanding the full price (and sometimes then some) of what a book was believed to be worth. Authors were notoriously bad business people, making the literary agent a vital intermediary in order to ensure a fair deal. Having a good idea of what would sell, agents frequently suggested book ideas to their clients, a practice that no doubt helped to shape the material being produced (and was instrumental in standardizing what ultimately appeared on bookshelves, some argued). Agents also often pushed for multi-book contracts with publishers, something that not only served writers' (and their own) interests but also created a climate of literary overproduction. The need to meet deadlines for a number of books over the course of a few years was said to reduce the quality of both fiction and nonfiction, making the literary agent heavily responsible for the fair chance that an author would have a very busy mill but little grist for it.[6]

One did not have to be an expert to notice that supply was exceeding demand within the publishing industry. "In no other country in the world is there such a torrent of writing," observed one journalist in

1940 after learning that his various neighbors in Los Angeles were spending their off-hours creating sonnets, short stories, one-act plays, and crime novels. An urgent need of cash was behind this writing mania, he believed, whether it was intended to be used to pay the installment on a new appliance, latest fashion, or doctor visit. With no investment required or simpler way to make money on the side, it made sense that writing was viewed as an attractive means of producing additional income. The phenomenal success of *Gone With the Wind*, both the novel and film, appeared to play a role in this literary frenzy among amateurs, as was the regular reporting of books being sold to Hollywood for tens of thousands of dollars.[7]

Even if one didn't have an epic saga of the Civil War to sell, there were other ways to make a quick buck with a clever piece of writing. Popular magazines were paying one, two, or even three dollars a word for short stories, this too a powerful incentive for bookkeepers, building contractors, dog trainers, insurance agents, and automobile mechanics to tap into their respective muse. "It is almost part of the American tradition, the 'American way of life,' that every family shall house at least one member who is by way of being a *litterateur*, major or minor," the reporter suggested, thinking that many people in this country suffered from *scribblitis*, a writing ailment that had reached epidemic proportions. Was it any surprise that hundreds of commercial schools promising to teach students "to write successfully in three weeks—with moneyback guarantee!" had sprung up across the country?[8]

The Gospel of Democracy

If fast cash was not forthcoming from *scribblitis*, there might be recognition from one's peers. Recognition was "very necessary to the writer," Pearl Buck believed, as it served as evidence that at least one other person found an author's work amusing, enlightening, or comforting.[9] Buck had won the Pulitzer Prize for fiction in 1932 for her *The Good Earth* and was awarded the Nobel Prize in Literature six years later, so she was well qualified to reflect on the importance of recognition for a writer. Prizes for writing, some including cash, were proliferating, with a good number being awarded to novels for a particular distinction. The Nobel and Pulitzer Prizes remained the most prestigious, but now there were prizes being given to novels written by authors from certain countries and by those in designated professions. There was a prize for first-time novelists and one for fiction writers under the age of thirty, all of this good news to American writers wanting some recognition for their hard work. Over a thousand novels were published every year but very few realized great commercial success, making the winning of a literary prize some compensation for the effort.[10]

Most exciting, perhaps, receiving one of the more important awards could very well land the lucky author a trip to New York City, with all expenses paid by the publisher. A series of interviews, dinners, and cocktail parties would likely follow after the announcement of the award, with the glitter of Manhattan sometimes known to make writers from the South or Midwest promptly relocate to Gotham where he or she would undoubtedly compose tangled stories of urban life. New Yorkers winning the same prize might go the other route by subletting his or her apartment and buying an eighteenth century cottage in Connecticut, having long dreamed of the tranquility to be found in country life. A pastoral novel about a man or woman who returned to his or her small town roots would then inevitably be produced, with writing sessions happily interrupted by regular watering of the garden and by the myriad of other chores that needed to be done to keep the old house standing.[11]

Unfortunately, the chances of a prize-winning first-time novelist striking gold with his or her second or third projects were not very good. A bright future appeared to beckon for a previously unpublished novelist who achieved a certain level of acclaim, as critics were apt to find the theme of his or her debut effort fresh and original (i.e., literally "novel"). Some authors found that they had precious little to say after having an initial hit, however, a hard revelation given that they had decided to become professional writers based on their early success. Such writers, especially if they had families to support (or perhaps multiple families if one was a divorced man), were now more or less committed to churning out work even if it was not of particularly high quality. Having a job and writing in one's spare time was an option for some, while others were in the fortunate position of having plenty of

Chapter 2 • The Realists, 1940–1959

money through inheritance or by marriage. (Proust and Tolstoy were two such lucky authors.) For those who were obligated to the trade, however, the realization that one's well was mostly dry was a major source of distress if not anguish. Turning to the somewhat easier and more reliable job of magazine fiction was typically the next step for these writers, their loss of prestige made up by the ability to keep a roof over their heads and their kids fed.[12]

Tapping into the intensifying patriotic spirit among Americans in some way was a good way for writers to receive a check in their mailbox. Even before Pearl Harbor, writers were encouraged to use their literary talents to fight dictatorships rooted in fascism and totalitarianism, making any piece extoling democracy something many magazine editors liked to see. Americans were strongly divided on the subject of getting involved in the European war, with many convinced that the nation would be better off to stay out of it. Others disagreed, however, seeing what was taking place overseas as a direct threat to the freedoms to be found in the United States. The latter group felt that writers could play an important role in convincing all Americans that they should not take a democratic form of government for granted. Because just one American out of five was believed to read a book a year (and just one in a hundred considered to be a "habitual" book reader, according to surveys), writers were urged to use other media—newspapers, magazines, radio, and pamphlets—to do their patriotic duty by reminding citizens of the blessings of liberty. "Spread the gospel of democracy," Norman Cousins, the executive editor of the *Saturday Review of Literature*, told writers in September 1940, seeing the non-book-reading public as a vital audience to reach for the country to defend itself against the rise of Hitlerism.[13]

The turmoil in Europe had a direct impact on the trajectory of the American writer in other important ways. European writers (and other artists) had begun arriving in this country in significant numbers through the late 1930s to escape religious, ethnic, or political persecution by the Nazis. Such authors forced into exile were "Hitler's gift to America," as *American Mercury* put it in 1943, a bounty that enriched the literary landscape of the United States.[14] Many writers who had experienced Nazi oppression firsthand joined previous émigrés and native-born Americans in producing what *Saturday Review of Literature* called in 1941 "manifestos of democracy," i.e., essays that Hitler himself should read to gain a better understanding of what this country was all about.[15] The flood of writers from Europe to America would help to shape publishing for decades to come, both on the author and editorial sides of the business, much like how exiled moviemakers from Germany permanently remade Hollywood.

With such clearly defined national mission, it was not at all surprising that the war had a major effect on the American writer and the material he or she decided to create. "Writers go to war," *Writer* magazine declared in 1942, as those with any literary talent were urged to contribute to the war effort by stringing together words that could unite Americans and motivate them to action.[16] "Words are weapons," announced *Independent Woman* the following year, as writers joined the fight to win the war and preserve the American Way of Life.[17] Whether covering the action from the front lines or producing propagandist material for the Office of War Information, writers were legitimately considered soldiers using Underwood typewriters rather than guns. (A good number of the writers in uniform for *Stars and Stripes*, the newspaper published by the Department of Defense, became successful journalists after the war.) Writers had many war-related themes to choose from, such as what books Americans had read during the last world war, and which authors had works banned (and sometimes burned) in Nazi Germany. Meanwhile, dime novels sold briskly on the home front as an escapist form of entertainment, and more highbrow readers enjoyed the great fiction still being published in the *New Yorker*. War may have been hell, but many American writers would later say that the early 1940s were the best years of their lives.

God's Gift to Publishers

Before, during, and after the war, it was commonly accepted that women accounted for the vast majority of books read in the United States. The belief that women were avid readers, much more so than men, persisted, to the degree that a saying in the industry was that females were "God's gift to publishers." John Erskine, an author and English professor, thought differently, arguing that women did indeed

Chapter 2 • The Realists, 1940–1959

buy books but usually didn't read them, and that the women who did read books often didn't buy them (having checked them out at the local library). Women especially didn't read bestsellers, he felt, although those were the most likely books for them to be carrying around. A bestseller served social purposes for women, Erskine argued, his rather misogynist view informed by personal experience. After being complimented by women attending author luncheons, Erskine had the habit of asking which part of his book was their favorite, a query that more often than not got zero response. "No slight upon women's intelligence is here implied," he wrote in the *Saturday Evening Post* in 1942, but "men, I think, will always take books more seriously than women."[18]

Erskine's theory aside, female-led literary societies and the book clubs in women's organizations were indeed of considerable value to both authors and publishers just as they had been before the war. Authors may have found the meet-and-greet portion of such events to be a painful experience, but most were more than happy to accept invitations to them because of the honorarium offered and the opportunity to sell (and sign) lots of books. The sequence and format of author luncheons rarely varied much. An author of a recently published book would receive an invitation from the chairperson of the entertainment committee of a society or club asking him or her to speak on any topic as long as some mention was made of the current literary scene. The author would then give a brief overview of his or her book along with some (usually neutral) commentary on others found on the "New" shelf of a bookstore. A handful of men might be in the audience, almost always on the insistence of their wives who were likely to be officials in the organization hosting the event. While they were glad to appear, they were even gladder to disappear. All authors agreed that the key to a successful lecture was saying "thank you" at the end of their talk, and quickly leaving the podium before any questions could be asked.[19]

Authors' reluctance to engage with an audience can be seen as one attempt to preserve some semblance of a private life. Writers' public and private lives tended to blur together, reflecting the mostly true idea that, even if not putting words on paper, they were still in some sense working. It was accepted that writers' minds never really turned off, as life itself provided the material for what might eventually be turned into a piece of literature. Because of this, writers were often looked to as experts in the art of life, a role they did not seek or for which they were particularly qualified.[20] Any and all advice was considered fair game to be sought by a reader from a writer, as if the former was sitting in a therapist's office or confession booth. The impact of a book could be so profound that it changed the way that readers saw the world, reason enough for them to ask its author if they should quit their jobs, leave their husbands, or make any other major life decision.[21]

Readers were apt to approach authors regarding more mundane matters. One author recalled receiving letters from readers over the course of his career asking if he knew how one could have a career in roller-skating, if he could name the best forty football and basketball players in the country, and, last but not least, if he could buy an oriental rug while overseas and send it to a woman upon his return (a money order for $1.50 was enclosed).[22] While requesting some sort of favor from an author was the norm, readers were known to also send them gifts of appreciation. Louise Dickinson Rich, a popular book-club author, recalled receiving a magnum of Champagne from one reader, and pecans, a wheel of Camembert cheese, and a tub of sherbet packed in dry ice from others. Letters from readers could also be quite moving, especially during the war when a book might serve an important purpose for members of the armed forces whose lives were in danger. Rich once received a joint letter from an entire Air Force squadron asking if the survivors could visit her after the war, quite a testament to the power of her words.[23]

Based on some of the impassioned writing during the war, it was easy to see how critics believed a golden age for literature was just around the corner. If nothing else, it appeared that all the suffering that had taken place for the last decade would give writers great empathy for the human condition that would somehow be made evident in both fiction and nonfiction. A more politically informed American writer would also emerge, many felt, this too a good thing for both publishers and readers. Best of all, perhaps, humor would reappear across the literary landscape, as much of the writing during the war was understandably less than sanguine. "It is a good profession to be an American writer," noted Harrison Smith, a contributing editor for the *Saturday Review of Literature* in June 1945, "and it will be even better in the future."[24]

There were other good reasons why writers or those wanting to join the profession were optimistic as it became clear that the Allies would win the war. One reason was that it appeared that the number of readers of books and magazines had increased during the war because of the broad-based desire to be better informed of world affairs. Seeing a big opportunity, publishers had already wisely decided to reprint classics and price them very affordably in order to tap into this new audience of readers. And with paper readily available again (there was a shortage during the war), new book and magazine publishers would like appear, another positive thing for postwar writers. Large media companies were eyeing what was now an industry generating hundreds of millions of dollars in sales, seeing publishing as a major source of revenue during the prosperous, leisure-driven postwar years. (Just three companies—Doubleday, Simon and Schuster, and World Publishing—dominated the business in 1945.) Publishers' advances had risen during the war, and Hollywood studios were paying more money than ever (up to $250,000) for books and plays that could be turned into blockbuster films. All in all, there was much to suggest that a writing career need not be a struggle for all but a few dozen A-listers. "Authors, good and bad, will be needed to fill millions of blank pages," Smith predicted, thinking that, "the intelligent writer who has to live in the proverbial garret will be hard to find."[25]

The Life of Man

A year after the war had ended, however, the rosy world of publishing had yet to appear, at least in terms of the quality of books being written. "No really great work has come out of the recent war yet," observed Paul Tabori in September 1946, proposing that, "the sense of proportion and the detachment of distance are still lacking." It would take some time to make some sense of the horrors that had taken place, many agreed, especially for artists wanting to translate their own experience in a creative medium. Interestingly, the same thing had happened after the First World War, until the modernists kicked into high gear in the early 1920s with their breakthrough form of fiction. Then and now literature tended to be journalistic in nature, as writers struggled to find a voice that was in sync with the new world order. "There is much groping and questioning, much uncertainty and uneasiness," Tabori, himself a journalist and author, added, as writers stuck to safe material about personalities and events in the headlines.[26]

Expecting there to be a burst of creative energy in publishing after the war, however, critics were puzzled by American writers' lack of vitality and originality. A decade earlier, writers like Hemingway, Steinbeck, Runyon, and John O'Hara had taken the literary scene by storm, and a decade before that the modernists achieved nothing less than having created a new art form. Now, "costume novels" were regularly appearing on bestseller lists, a source of angst for devotees of "real" literature. Even worse for intellectuals, attractive women tended to be the authors of these books, something publishers were eager to exploit in advertising. In this genre, the "adventures of a tempestuous heroine of easy virtue," as one critic described the literary form, were related, with sexuality, if there was any doubt, the underlying theme. (Some of these novels, whose book jackets usually featured a busty woman depicted in the foreground and a ship in the distance, were actually banned in Boston.) Some nonfiction, especially biographies of American historical figures were also quite popular, but these books too leaned more towards entertainment than serious scholarship. While there obviously was always a business side to publishing, eggheads resented the loss of art in literature and the "Hollywoodization" of books in the United States. If it meant more readers, however, was it necessarily a bad thing that books had become a cleverly packaged and heavily advertised product aimed for a mass market?[27]

Perhaps so, if Americans' favorite literary genre really did center around loose women being chased across the Caribbean by rough-and-tumble scalawags. True or otherwise, the consensus was that the late forties was a less than stellar period for the American novel if only for the cookie-cutter approach that now defined the fiction being published. The best known novelists, i.e., Hemingway, Dos Passos, Faulkner, Robert Penn Warren, John Marquand, Katherine Anne Porter, and William Saroyan, were all at work on something or taking a break, leaving a vacuum of sorts in fiction at the time. One reason for this was the lack of a guiding style for authors to follow, the "Hemingway school" (in which morality was questioned and violence and death heavily featured) seemingly having run its course. The drift of some authors to Hollywood was also blamed for the dip in quality. (Faulkner had taken to raising corn and cotton on his farm in Oxford, Mississippi, and was writing for the movies, he explained, "only when I run out of money.") For a novelist, however, screenwriting drained one's ideas and originality, many felt, and was thus a dangerous practice if one wanted to continue writing fiction. One another factor was what Dos Passos called "the best-seller system and the book clubs which tend to standardize reading tastes on a mediocre level," each of these also commodifying what most believed should have been an inventive and creative process.[28]

While Dos Passos, along with Hemingway, were generally considered the only modernist writers to still be producing work that was anything close to what they had in the 1920s, they and their contemporaries cast a large shadow over the postwar literary scene. Why had history not repeated itself after the Second World War with the emergence of a new, groundbreaking movement of literature? While the nation's current crop of young novelists had also come through a calamitous war, the answer went, there was little of the disillusionment that the Lost Generation had experienced and had relied upon as the existential backbone of their stories. As well, from a purely technical standpoint, writers such as Dos Passos, Hemingway, Fitzgerald, and E.E. Cummings had devised a new literary language by which to tell their stories, while post–World War II novelists had yet to come up with an equivalent set of innovative methods to employ in their own work.[29]

The sheer radicalness of the modernists made even the cream of the crop of postwar fiction seem frothy and inconsequential. Novels by such authors as Norman Mailer, Truman Capote, Gore Vidal, and Tennessee Williams were certainly interesting, critics pointed out, but they were not revolutionary in that they borrowed upon the literary style conceived by the modernists. The earlier generation had "turned the American myth upside down," noted Harrison Smith, "with "nothing resembling this literary revolution occurring anywhere else in the world."[30] While arguably better written, contemporary novels simply lacked the impact of those published between the wars. "Their finish is more often that of a machine-made, prefabricated product than of a finely wrought piece of craftsmanship," wrote John W. Aldridge in 1949, describing midcentury American fiction writers as the "uneasy inheritors of a revolution."[31]

Most apparent in contemporary novels, perhaps, was the lack of condemnation about some aspect of American life that had been such a defining element of the modernists' work. Sherwood Anderson's *Winesburg, Ohio* (1919) and Sinclair Lewis's *Main Street* (1920) and *Babbitt* (1924) each exposed the futility of middle-class existence, for example, and Theodore Dreiser's *An American Tragedy* (1925) was an indictment of sorts of the entire nation's way of life. With the Depression, a love for America emerged as a principal theme in fiction and poetry (and in art and music), this marking the end of the literary era steeped in satire and protest. Willa Cather, Edna Ferber, Thomas Wolfe, Carl Sandburg, and Archibald MacLeish were just some writers to celebrate American life in the 1930s, an approach that nicely fed into the patriotic spirit during the Second World War. Now, however, there seemed to be a void in American literature, with little of the critical dimension of the 1920s or the celebratory quality of the 1930s to be found in fiction.[32]

While some critics believed that their colleagues were being too hard on the current generation of novelists ("They are now busy producing a forceful and imaginative literature," Smith argued, seeing postwar writers' existential despair and critique of America's contradictions as equivalent in some ways to that of the modernists), the general consent was that nothing could match the body of work created by the Lost Generation.[33] Some blamed the beginnings of the Cold War and its cultural consequences for postwar fiction being in the doldrums. Pervasive anti–Communist and anti–Soviet sentiment had created a gloomy literary climate, these critics argued, making sales of (often badly written) novels drop precipitously. Publishers were responding by cutting back their fiction lists, not good news for veteran or aspiring novelists. Writers appeared to be affected by the loss of individualism in American society at mid-century, as seemingly

Chapter 2 • The Realists, 1940–1959

all-powerful institutions—the government, the military, and large corporations—crushed out some of the creative spirit of artists. (Jazz and modern art seemed to be doing fine, it should be noted.) American writers had "lost that clarity of vision which is a prerequisite to successful literary composition," thought C. Hartley Grattan in 1951, positing that the current wave of novelists no longer knew "what the life of man is all about."[34]

A Kind of Disease

Whether they possessed a deep understanding of life or otherwise, many writers felt they had no choice but to put words down on paper. Real writers wrote, whether or not their material would ever be seen by anyone else, with this urge sometimes becoming a compulsion. "The desire to write novels sometimes seems to me a kind of disease," thought R.C. Hutchinson in 1949, something that "afflicted many people, either early or late in life." While most such people made a recovery, some were not so fortunate. Some writers believed they contacted the disease very early in life when being read to as a toddler. It intensified during writers' teenage years as they created their own material, and got yet worse when first published. From that point a cure was unlikely, as authors had by then acquired a virulent strain of the writing bug.[35] If some writers suffered from some sort of literary affliction or addiction, the same could be said of particularly avid readers and collectors of books. "Bibliophilism" was the latter's affliction, with those who had contracted the condition seemingly unable to stop consuming and accumulating books much the same way that certain writers could not stop producing them.[36]

Rather than be born as natural writers, however, most professionals learned the craft by trial and error, with working out the technical kinks typically a long process. (Less could very well be more, some novelists painfully learned after writing books of over 100,000 words.) After learning the art of storytelling, more ambitious writers strove to take their work to a higher level. A major leap took place when a writer elevated his or her work beyond that of pleasant entertainment or an interesting diversion for the reader. Realizing such an

51

achievement meant that the author had written something truly meaningful, and that the work would likely be read for decades because it conveyed some enduring, often philosophical aspect of the human experience. The sometimes ambiguous relationship between good and evil was one such theme, explaining why so many authors throughout history had chosen it when deciding what their next book should be about.[37]

Achieving what could be seen as an ultimate goal for authors was especially difficult for those writing part-time. The need to keep a day job and write a paragraph or two when one had a little free time was generally not a good formula to produce one's best work, much less one that would be judged a classic.[38] As well, changes in the publishing business after the war were working against those who were not established authors. The cost to launch a commercially successful book in 1950 was much greater than in 1930 or 1940, a fact that made publishers take on fewer new writers. Sticking to "safe" authors, i.e., those who already had a solid record in terms of previous sales (at least 5,000–10,000 copies per book), was now part of the business, not good news for those trying to sell their first novel or work of nonfiction .[39] The "millions of blank pages" that would have to be filled had yet to materialize, making the first five years of the postwar era less than a golden age for the American writer.

Another new aspect of the business was publishers' expectation for authors to promote their books by making numerous personal appearances. Movie stars had for some time been contracted to plug a film in conjunction with its release, but now authors were expected to make the rounds to generate publicity. Authors' first job was to speak at publishers' conferences in order to get sales reps excited about the new product and, after its publication, do a series of radio interviews to get the public interested. Television interviews also were an option, as long as the author's physical appearance was not too off-putting. Meeting with journalists from the print media was next to try to get the book reviewed, hopefully in the *New York Times, New-York Tribune, Time, Newsweek,* and *Variety*. Finally, authors were urged to hit the road to speak and sign books at bookstores, literary teas and lunches, and book fairs, quite an exhausting and time-consuming enterprise. Most of the country's leading writers, including Hemingway, Faulkner,

Chapter 2 • The Realists, 1940–1959

O'Hara, and John Hersey, refused to engage in such marketing practices, a decision that did not seem to effect sales of their books or the chances of their winning a major prize.[40]

The new constraints and demands being imposed on authors was no deterrent for unpublished writers to try to join the club. It was difficult to think of an occupation in which more people wanted to be employed despite the shaky-at-best economics. And unlike most jobs, most writers refused to give up their dream of becoming a bona fide author. Aspiring carpenters would try something else when it became apparent they were all thumbs, for example, and those planning to be doctors would choose a different path if they realized the sight of blood made them dizzy. But many writers would keep at it, often for decades, by taking courses, going to conferences, and relentlessly submitting material to anyone and everyone who might be helpful in turning a manuscript into a book. What was it about writing that drove people to such extreme lengths to succeed? No one could say for sure (one Freudian-trained doctor had recently claimed that writing was the symptom of a psychological trauma experienced by infants),[41] but there seemed to be no slowdown in the number of Americans who wanted to see their names in print.[42]

An easier and increasingly common path for writers to do what they loved for a living was to work for a large company. Writers were very much a part of the expansion of Big Business in the 1950s, with more of them becoming salaried employees. "The status of the writer is shifting, at an accelerating pace, from that of an independent creator to that of a wage-earner," noted the playwright Elmer Rice in 1952. Writers were flocking to media companies and advertising agencies and public relations firms in droves, with many others taking government jobs. Receiving a weekly paycheck was something writers were not at all used to; the stability of having a guaranteed income as long as one held the job was, to put it mildly, a refreshing experience. The ability to retire at age sixty-five with a pension was like a dream come true for people used to getting paid by the word. This shift was historic in scope. For more than a century now, craft had been disappearing in America, with writing part of this gradual trend towards standardization and industrialization in virtually dimension of everyday life. Would the writer as we knew him or her even be around in another century?

"The relative independence of the book writer and the playwright is precarious [and] may, perhaps, be doomed," Rice fretted, worried that the profession was starting to look a lot like Henry Ford's assembly line.[43]

Small Stories

In this kind of corporatized literary climate, it was not surprising that a good many writers who had the means periodically left the United States for creative inspiration. For a real writer versus one who, as Tennessee Williams diplomatically put it in 1950, "adopted the vocation as a convenient social pose to excuse his predilection for various kinds of waywardness," where one chose to work remained an important consideration. Williams was of the mind that most writers, even Americans, were romanticists, and thus looked to Europe for stimulation given that there was precious little romance to now be found in the United States (a wisp of it could still be detected in New Orleans and San Francisco, he felt). Paris had been a great spot for expatriates like Hemingway, Fitzgerald, and many others to write before the Second World War but, for Williams, the city had lost its magic. American writers still flocked to the cafes on the Left Bank, hoping perhaps to be inspired by Sartre or Camus, but most were actually there for the "waywardness" that could be found in abundance on La Rive Gauche. (Many such writers didn't haul out their typewriters until mid-afternoon, having overindulged in some form of merriment the previous night.) It was Rome, specifically Via Veneto, that was the far better choice for writers like himself who wanted to get some work done, he believed, finding the warmth there, both literally and among the people, well suited to arouse one's muse.[44]

Whatever Williams's geographic formula was for producing original material (he used Manhattan as his home base but frequented Key West in the winter), it certainly was working despite his various personal demons. The playwright of *The Glass Menagerie* and *A Streetcar Named Desire* was one of just a handful of American writers to be taking real risks, something that did not go unnoticed by leaders of the literary community. The pressures of conformity appeared to be playing a part in the lackluster work of the postwar years, a source of frustration

Chapter 2 • The Realists, 1940–1959

for publishers seeking material that was somehow dissident or defiant. "There are no great rebels, no mavericks, no iconoclasts," observed Harold Strauss, editor-in-chief of Knopf in 1952, thinking the lack of inspiration was a result of writers living in "an age of muted voices." While American writers had achieved great technical skill, they feared taking on ambitious projects, he believed, with too many authors content with telling "small stories." (Ralph Ellison's *Invisible Man*, which was published that year by Random House and won the National Book Award for Fiction in 1953, was a rare exception.) Based on the manuscripts that crossed his own desk, Strauss felt that current authors spent too much time writing and not enough reading, going as far as to collectively label them "illiterate." A greater familiarity with the classics, or even the works of relatively recent authors such as Henry James, Edith Wharton, F. Scott Fitzgerald, and Willa Cather, would go a long way towards providing contemporary writers with the capacity to bring forth exceptional literature.[45]

If readers had the same, not very flattering opinion of writers as Strauss, they might have been a lot more comfortable when meeting one. Many readers simply did not know how to behave with writers of some renown, making a kind of tutorial necessary. Knowing a certain author would be at a get-together they were also planning to attend, readers (or non-readers, in this case) often went to a library to skim one of his or her books, under the false assumption that the writer would want only to talk shop. Discussing one's own book was actually the last thing authors wanted to do a party, Louis Auchincloss explained in 1954, especially with a total stranger. (Painters and musicians were the same, while actors were known to talk about their latest project with anyone and everyone.) Auchincloss also recommended avoiding the obvious when meeting an author. Authors could be asked a dozen times at a social gathering whether they used a pen, pencil, typewriter, or one of those newfangled electric typewriters, making that question (as well as why contemporary writers chose such "unpleasant" topics to write about) something better left unsaid.[46]

There were other "don'ts" for readers planning to chat up an author at a soiree, according to Auchincloss (who ultimately wrote over sixty books and received the National Medal of Arts from President George W. Bush). Asking the titles of his or her books was a no-no, as authors found having to mention them in public somewhat embarrassing. The need to provide a ten-second recap of one's latest work was also awkward, yet "What's it about?" was often the follow-up question once guests knew the title. Strangely, individuals who had not read any of an author's books felt compelled to inform him or her of that fact, as if this confession was something required to begin a conversation. Others were known to make it clear to authors that they did not read the entire genre in which the author operated, thinking this too was vital information that had to be disclosed.[47]

The other end of the spectrum in author etiquette was when readers gushed when meeting one they particularly admired. More often than not a middle-aged woman, the gusher assumed the gushee liked to receive large quantities of enthusiastic praise, this too usually not true, especially when delivered in high volume and in close quarters. Finally, Auchincloss let readers know that it was bad form for them to critique an author's work, something that occurred with surprising regularity at cocktail parties. Such commentary (often preceded by the disclaimer that, "I'm no literary critic, but"), was especially despised by authors, as it was almost certain that they either vehemently disagreed or were already fully aware of the flaws in their book, having heard same from reviewers, friends, or family.[48]

Auchincloss's advice was valuable if only because one was more likely to meet an author at a party than in decades past. There were 16,000 professional authors in the United States, according to the 1950 census, 3,000 more than in 1940. Only a couple hundred, however, earned the majority of their income by writing hardcover books, with the remainder authors of textbooks, juveniles (books for children and teens), and pulps (most of them mysteries or westerns). Advances averaged $1,000 to $2,000 in 1954 and royalty rates were lower than what they once were, partly explaining why there were so few full-time authors. As well, Hollywood was now buying fewer stories and paying less for them, reducing the chances that a writer would hit the jackpot. Publishers were increasingly shying away from fiction, seeing the bigger opportunity in subjects that readers would find more practical. Sales of nonfiction books now exceeded fiction by about three times, in fact, making the dream of writing the proverbial Great American Novel even more remote.[49]

While selling at least 5,000 copies of a book was likely to be enough for an author to remain one, the mass-market orientation of the business pushed publishers to actively seek out potential bestsellers. For financial reasons, selling 12,000 copies of a book had become the goal of major publishers in the 1950s, with authors who achieved that mark the beneficiaries of special attention. Regular lunches with one's editor at expensive restaurants was one perk, with lavish launch parties for the lucky author's next books another. Authors of books that sold less than that magic number were treated respectfully by their publisher, but could expect to eat lunch on their own. Like today, most books published sixty years ago lost money, making it vitally important for publishers to get the occasional hit to stay in business. Also like now, an author's first book was considered very important, as its relative success often set the stage for his or her remaining literary career.[50]

An American Language

Indeed, first-time novelists seemed determined to make a mark with their debut effort, often producing deeply personal works steeped in psychology. Through the 1950s, writers explored their inner selves, plumbing the depths of their conscious and unconscious minds. Not coincidentally, psychoanalysis was all the rage, even more so than in the 1920s when it was first embraced by writers. The cultural elite was especially keen on discovering what made the human animal tick, a curiosity that heavily informed novels of the period. If the great American writers of the 1920s and 1930s were part of the disillusioned and alienated Lost Generation, those of the postwar years were considered to be the Anxious Generation, interested in venting their neuroses through their art form. Foreigners were puzzled by what were labeled "obsessive novels," while critics in this country worried that this new school of "personalism" accurately reflected American society. If so, the United States was a truly sick place, they argued, especially when it came to the so-called sexual "depravity" to be found in a good number of novels being published (and eagerly read).

Anxious or otherwise, a fair number of writers found receptive audiences during the postwar years despite critics' (and some publishers') general dissatisfaction with the fiction being written. Harper Lee, Saul Bellow, J.D. Salinger, Norman Mailer, Sylvia Plath, Joseph Heller, John Updike, Philip Roth, and Ralph Ellison were just some American writers whose work could be found on many a bookshelf. Translations of works of both fiction and nonfiction were increasing in number, a clear sign of an expanding global market for American writing. While a new breed of young novelists engaged in social criticism by examining life in the margins, especially in urban "slums," others focused on the abundant demand for juvenile literature, short stories, and magazine articles. Exposing the underbelly of placid postwar life, particularly that in the suburbs, was prime fodder for intellectual writers such as James Thurber and Peter de Vries who each used *The New Yorker* as their literary home base. Throughout the fifties, writers in this country were either purposely or unintentionally moving "toward an American language," as *Atlantic* expressed it in 1952, something that had been vigorously pursued ever since the modernists emerged from the literary shadow of England.[51] The following year, Van Wyck Brooks argued in his book *The Writer in America* that authors in this country were attempting to go "beyond adolescence," this too a much sought-after achievement.[52]

Much like between the wars, there was also considerable interest in writers themselves, with many wondering who went into the peculiar profession and for what reasons. Were writers born to write?, some asked, suggesting that there was a specific and inherent personality attached to the job. Americans generally held a polarized view of writers, either conjuring up the image of the starving artist who was believed to have died broke (e.g., O. Henry or Edgar Allan Poe) or, conversely, the one who had made a fortune spinning wildly popular tales of adventure (e.g., Zane Grey). The reality, of course, was much less interesting than this seemingly contrary picture of literary feast or famine. Most American writers at mid-century were part of the great middle class, neither desperate for something to eat or using a gold-plated typewriter to spill out their latest bestseller. Prolific authors of textbooks, juveniles, mysteries, and westerns could make a nice living as a full-time writer, but they were more the exception than the rule. The couple of hundred Americans who consistently earned most of their income from writing hardcover books were in a class by

Chapter 2 • The Realists, 1940–1959

themselves, making a genuine author of either fiction or nonfiction quite a rare find. The scarcity of full-time writers was reflected in the available data. The 16,184 Americans (6,235 women) who had called themselves authors in the 1950 census had an average reported income of $3,000 ($31,500 in 2017 dollars), about the same as an entry-level bank teller at the time.[53]

While the publishing business was holding its own, it had hardly become the financial juggernaut that large media companies believed it would soon after the war. Twice as many works of fiction were published in the mid–1950s as a half-century earlier, but more than half of contemporary novels did not sell at least 5,000 copies in bookstores, that number usually considered the financial break-even point. Just a couple dozen novels would now sell 50,000 copies in a year, making it understandable why there were so few truly successful authors. Worse news was that the standard royalty rate of 20 percent paid to authors between the wars had by 1955 shrunk to about 12 percent, making it even tougher for the vast majority of writers to quit their day jobs. Versus an average advance ($1,500, or about $14,000 in today's dollars) or royalties, the bigger money to made by authors was from book club sales, paperback reprints, and, again, serialization in magazines or newspapers. Extending one's material into other forms of entertainment, i.e., film, radio, television, or Broadway, was the only real chance at a bonanza for most writers, with novels seen less and less as a stand-alone product and more and more as a multimedia vehicle.[54]

When viewing the profession of writing in the United States, then, it was more accurate to see it primarily as the domain of those working part-time in the field (half of whom lived in New York City or its suburbs). The relatively few full-time authors may have represented the literary elite, but there was no shame attached to splitting one's time with other jobs in order to keep afloat as long as one could still produce quality work. America had a long and proud tradition with part-time writers, for one thing (Herman Melville was a customs inspector on the New York docks when he wrote *Moby Dick*), and some of the country's best and brightest minds (e.g., Lionel Trilling, Wallace Stegner, and Katherine Anne Porter) taught when not working on a book. Others edited magazines or journals, obviously a natural fit for many writers. As well, part-time writers who had expertise in a certain field were well suited for works of nonfiction, an area that continued to be in increasing demand among publishers. Discovering the next Great American Novel remained the Holy Grail among many editors, but how-to and self-help books often sold briskly, making them the bread and butter for many publishers. Dieticians, gardeners, clergymen, and psychoanalysts were making a pretty penny by following the time-tested wisdom to write what one knew and, as a bonus, expanding their reputation as authorities in their respective field.[55]

Despite the maturation of the publishing business and the mainstreaming of the American writer, the profession was still occasionally viewed as the province of eccentrics. (Anyone reading the letters or diaries of notable novelists of the past—Gustave Flaubert or Virginia Woolf, for example—would likely reach the same conclusion.) Self-absorption—that writers believed the world revolved around them and their work—was viewed as the principal hazard of the field. Egotism was simply part and parcel of the business, many agreed, just as a toolkit was to a handyman. If writers just kept to themselves, this would not be a problem. But writers had relationships with other people, which is where their personality quirks became an issue. Friends and family had to expect a certain aloofness and remoteness, as novelists directed their emotional sides to the characters within the fictional worlds they created. As in the 1930s, special warning was directed to women considering marrying a writer. "If you throw in your lot with his you too will be drawn into the orbit of his struggle and, although you may share some of his moments of happiness, you will not be able to escape his wounds," Benedict Thielen cautioned a girl about to be wed to a writer in *Harper's Magazine* in 1955, urging her to run while she still had the chance.[56]

The Disorganization Man

Despite the lingering doubts about their emotional health, the prospects of the American writer had improved significantly over the past decade. The late fifties were generally good times for writers of all sorts as the reading public remained keen on nonfiction and expressed

Chapter 2 • The Realists, 1940–1959

renewed interest in novels. It was "bullish days for fictioneers," one publication declared in 1955, as authors engaged in what *Nation* described in 1957 as "slick sociology."[57] Symbolism had become recognized as the dominant style of fiction in the country, a means to express resistance from or anger at the "system" and its pressure to conform to social norms without being attacked as anti–American. Nearly everyone, especially the literati, were positively fascinated by the Beats in San Francisco who, much like the modernists, appeared to be creating nothing less than a new art form. In New York City, meanwhile, writers trying to make it were, as always, scribbling by day and working nights (or vice versa) to pay the (still affordable) rent. If struggling actors in Gotham were waiting tables, aspiring authors were known to drive taxies in the wee hours to stay afloat until their big break. Life was appropriately considered the raw material for art, after all, making hours spent with total strangers in a cab a prime opportunity to gather potentially lucrative stories.

Even with the apparent turnaround of the novel, the jury was essentially out when it came to how fiction of the period would likely be canonized. By 1957, it was clear that the generation of writers who had come of age after the Second World War would never be seen as equal in stature to the group who had appeared on the scene after the First World War. Forces beyond their control had shaped the former's literary sensibilities, critics concluded, essentially making them victims of the economic and social turmoil of the 1930s and early 1940s. Postwar writers (and all adults, for that matter) were perceived as being old before their time, having spent their youthful years in the dark days of the Depression and wartime. The pressures of domesticity—to get married, have children, and move to a house in the suburbs to be filled with the creature comforts now to be had—added to the likelihood for postwar writers to prioritize stability over creativity. The constant threat of nuclear apocalypse and end of civilization deepened the anxieties of this generation, and served as an impetus for them to look to security wherever they could find it. Writers of the late fifties were "intellectuals in gray flannel suits," stated Raymond Walters, Jr., book review editor for the magazine renamed *The Saturday Review*, these men and women not likely to challenge the status quo like the modernists had between the wars.[58]

Another group of writers, however, was already separating themselves from the Anxious Generation and mainstream American society as a whole. If postwar writers had become "organization men," the Beat Generation (or simply "Beats") represented the "disorganization man," as *Time* magazine labeled them in 1958. (Jack Kerouac officially coined the phrase the "Beat Generation" in 1948, although the term "Beats" had been used earlier by the group and carried both negative and positive connotations.) With the possible exception of Britain's "Angry Young Men," the Beats, who had met years earlier around Columbia University, represented the most discussed literary movement of the late 1950s. An intense restlessness defined the Beats (both their writing and their actual lives), making some wonder if they were on a search for meaning or attempting to flee from it. The protagonists in works by Kerouac, Allen Ginsberg, Clellon Holmes, and a handful of others appeared to be in a constant state of euphoria or despair, reflective of what the authors claimed to be a mystical quest for a divine entity. Sex, alcohol, and drugs helped to fuel the "hipster" character's journey, with sensation and a focus on the self considered to be the only remaining safe havens in a world that could be blown up at any time.[59]

Although the quality of their work was questioned (*Time* considered it to be "semi-literate"), the Beats captured the imagination of a nation frozen within the intense conformity of the Cold War years. Kerouac's *On the Road*, which had been published in 1957, was the group's unofficial manifesto, filled with ideas and a writing style that would never have been found in the "neurotic" works of the postwar novelists. "We gotta go and never stop going till we get there," uttered a hipster in the book, the destination unsure but his energy never in doubt. Their family lives and relationships unfulfilling, to say the least, the central characters in the Beats' novels were on a mission to find something—anything, actually—to which they could relate. Ginsberg's impassioned poem "Howl" had also struck a chord with the reading public who had never read a sentence quite like, "I saw the best minds of my generation destroyed by madness, starving hysterical naked, dragging themselves through the negro streets at dawn looking for an angry fix." Many critics were skeptical of the Beats' oeuvre (J. Donald Adams of the *New York Times* quipped that Ginsberg's poem published

Chapter 2 • The Realists, 1940–1959

in 1956 should have been titled *Bleat*), but it could not be argued that no movement had a bigger, if relatively brief, impact on the country's literary scene since the 1920s.[60]

Perhaps the most remarkable thing about the Beats is that they appeared to have no desire to change the system, as members of countercultural movements often do. Leftist writers, notably Norman Mailer, aligned themselves with the Beats if only as a convenient means of separation from the "Squares." But it was postwar novelists like Mailer, Wright Morris, Saul Bellow, Carson McCullers, J.D. Salinger, and Flannery O'Connor who were more likely to be remembered, according to Granville Hicks, with nothing of real, long-term value to learn from the Beats. It was the individual's search for identity, transformation of the self, quest for wisdom, and concept of evil that novelists of the late 1940s and 1950s had so firmly committed themselves to, he argued, and it was these rich philosophical themes that offered substance for serious readers of fiction. Going further, Hicks challenged other critics' claim that postwar American authors wrote books that were not bold or "big" enough, finding the "quietness" of their work both reassuring and rewarding.[61]

While critics debated the lasting significance of the Beats and of the larger generation of postwar novelists, an occasional voice served as a compelling reminder of the importance of writers. "In my view, the world is led by men who write," Larston D. Farrar told a crowd in Houston in 1959, thinking writers were more influential in shaping society than politicians, who were generally considered to have the bigger impact on other people's lives. Historically speaking, Farrar, author of such books as *Successful Writers and How They Work* and *How to Make $18,000 a Year Free Lance Writing*, had a valid point. A good many Biblical figures, as well as Aristotle, Tolstoy, Marx, and Voltaire were all writers, as were most of the Founding Fathers. Writers' primary role was to help others understand what was currently taking place and offer potential solutions to problems, he told the staff of the Houston Public Library and members of the Houston Scribblers Club, making their mission a truly noble one. Although one could argue with Farrar's thesis (Americans spent three times as much money on alcoholic beverages in 1958 than on reading material, i.e., newspapers, magazines, and books), there was no doubt that writers were playing a key role in parsing the political and economic dynamics of the Cold War and in bringing attention to the nation's social ills.[62] The American writer was poised to take a much different turn, however, and in the process forge a new chapter in their own fascinating history.

CHAPTER 3

The Intellectuals, 1960–1979

> *"The young man who announces to his family that he wishes to become a writer rather than a broker ... is far less likely to be thrown out of the house than he would have been a generation or two ago."*
> —Harvey Swados, 1965

For a few days in May 1978, a group of some of the best-known American writers sat across a table from a contingent of notable Soviet writers in New York City. The writers, which included Edward Albee, Arthur Miller, Joyce Carol Oates, John Updike, and Kurt Vonnegut from the American side, had gathered to discuss literary matters, but the meeting, held a couple of years before the collapse of the Soviet Union, obviously had political overtones. Mixed in with discussions about the art of the novel and the role of the author in the global literary community were conversations that addressed the issues of Soviet dissident writers and the dearth of books by Russian authors that were published in the United States. The summit was actually a sequel to a similar one held a year previously in Moscow. Then too American and Soviet writers chatted amiably about such bookish topics as the challenges of being creative in a complex world, how to bring fictional characters to life, and how literature could contribute to human potential, all against the backdrop of the latter day Cold War.[1]

Such high-level meetings, patterned after conferences held between top government officials, reflected the new kind of cultural status that the American writer now wielded. Through the 1960s and 1970s, writers shed much of their oddball image and became recognized as key figures on the American scene. More so than ever before, writers were viewed as intellectuals, their views on the current issues of the day valued for being quite literally the smartest people in the room. For the average writer, making a living though one's words was as tough as ever, but leading authors made gads of money and enjoyed the kind of fame usually limited to movie stars. Writers were at the center of the social turbulence of those two decades, and entered the political fray in a way that previous generations of authors never dared to. While some argued that the Great American Novel had become less than great, the American writer was at the top of his or her game at this critical juncture in the nation's history.

The Muddled Mind of Man

Much of writers' newfound prestige rooted in intelligence had much to do with the general health of the American publishing industry. As the Kennedys moved into the White House, the book business was doing quite well, a reflection of the still robust postwar economy. More books were being published and more readers were buying them, a positive thing for everyone involved in the industry, including writers. Critics argued that some degree of overall quality had been sacrificed with greater quantity, however, as the race for increased sales demanded that a certain number of substandard books be published. Still, a long view suggested that the business had come a long way over the past three decades. Sales of fiction in 1959 were slightly higher than in 1929, with the real growth coming in nonfiction. Twice as many business, sports, law, science, and technical books were each sold in 1959 than in 1929, good news for writers specializing in a practical or professional subject.[2]

The institutionalization of the American writer that had begun in the 1950s continued in the early 1960s. In addition to corporations, foundations and the federal government were hiring more writers, making some think the profession had been largely co-opted by what was becoming known as the Establishment. A certain segment of the literary set was not happy to see writers move out of their Greenwich Village walkups upon taking a middle-class, nine-to-five job, seeing it as a violation of the creative-person-as-starving-artist mythology. Although they were glad to accept almost any paid position to supplement their income as authors, it was silly to think that writers who agreed to work for the government or some other large bureaucratic organization instantly became conformists. Saul Bellow, Mary McCarthy, Ralph Ellison, Alfred Kazin, and Mark Harris had all recently gone on missions for the Department of State as cultural ambassadors, for example, but they each seemed to be as critical of government policies as ever.[3]

Taking part- or full-time jobs appeared not to diminish writers' literary output. Whether to earn money, attract attention, or simply satisfy some kind of primal urge to tell a story, writers were showing no sign of slowing down in the early 1960s. About 15,000 new books were being published annually in the United States, a quantity large enough to suggest that anyone having what he or she believed was a good idea to try to get published. The numbers, however, were deceiving. Just one in ten books sold enough copies to make publishers any money, meaning their authors would earn no royalties after receiving what was likely to be a minimal advance. Those seeing their name in print, even if it did mean having been paid very little money for a great deal of time, were the lucky ones. Ten books for every one that actually got published were written, it was believed, making one question the wisdom, if not sanity, of the whole enterprise.[4]

Even the relatively rare achievement of publication often proved to be disappointing. Having long dreamed of getting published, first-time authors likely expected their book to have considerably more success than what actually took place in most occasions. Authors were not unusually surprised to find that the day their book was published turned out to be like any other day. The publisher might send an author a telegram of congratulations, but this could be the only sign of recognition that the book now existed. Friends were oblivious that their buddy was now a published author, and even one's spouse usually needed reminding that the big day had arrived. Reviews would trickle in over the following weeks or months, but it was not likely that the author's life had been altered in any significant way. Six months after publication, the author would receive a royalty statement that added no joy to the experience. An average 2,000 copies were likely to have been sold to bookstores, with about 500 returned to the publisher for credit. The earned royalty in this typical scenario was $750 but the author probably had received an advance of roughly $2,000, meaning no more money would be forthcoming. "This gloomy progression of events is reproduced several thousand times each year," noted Paul R. Reynolds, a well known literary agent, estimating the average author's rate of pay for writing his or her book as $4 an hour.[5]

Based on its own level of acceptance rate and pay, magazine writing was equally gloomy. *The Saturday Evening Post*, which remained a potentially lucrative publishing opportunity for freelance writers, received an average of three thousand unsolicited articles every week, out of which two or three were likely to be accepted. One or two of the six hundred or so articles sent to the *Atlantic Monthly* every month would be published, with the acceptance rate of other popular magazines quite similar. For the average writer, neither book nor magazine publishing presented what any reasonable person would consider to be a good business proposition based on its probable financial return. "If writing is a business," Robert L. Oliver, a professor at Penn State, told an audience in 1961, "it seems obviously to be one of the most inefficient businesses the muddled mind of man ever conceived."[6]

Given the number of Americans scribbling away whenever they could, there had to be other, non-financial reasons why people wanted to call themselves writers. Whether or not it was a conscious decision, some writers pursued publication so fervently because it offered the possibility of immortality. One's work survived beyond oneself, after all, making a paper trail of books, magazine articles, or other forms of writing a tangible legacy. The thought that someone fifty years after one's death might check out from a library a book that one had written likely kept many individuals working despite the lottery-like odds of getting published and the usually paltry money to be made if one was lucky enough to beat those odds. Other forms of validation—say, seeing a copy of one's book in a shop window or getting a letter from someone who found reading one's work a profound experience—were also perfectly rational reasons to commit oneself to the otherwise irrational endeavor of writing.[7]

At least one notable American writer appeared to have no need at all for external validation. J.D. Salinger's appearance on the cover of *Time* magazine in October 1961 was ironic (and no doubt undesired) as the author was arguably most famous for not wanting to be famous. His collection of short stories, *Franny and Zooey*, had just been published, and was riding on the success of his 1951 novel *The Catcher in the Rye*, which remained enormously popular, especially among young people. Salinger's determined attempt at obscurity was rare for any artist, including writers whose success typically relied on a certain amount of fame. Norman Mailer, for example, would have perhaps killed for such tremendous publicity (he had stabbed his wife recently at a party, which made headlines), but Salinger wished to be as anonymous as possible. Americans were surprised and fascinated by the novelist's insistence to stay under the radar at a time when public relations was being used more than ever to construct and market personalities to the mass media in order to increase the visibility of clients. William Faulkner was known for being extremely private, but Salinger had taken the desire to be left alone to an entirely new level, challenging the accepted notion that a public figure should naturally want to be in the public eye.[8]

Shiny, New, Professional Horizons

Eschewing publicity (but getting it nonetheless) broke one of the cardinal rules toward achieving the primary goal of most publishers and authors: a bestseller. Based on sales reports from bookstores (which could often be quite inaccurate), a few publications, notably the *New York Times*, issued a weekly bestseller list that garnered much attention in the industry. There was no tried and true formula for producing a bestseller, of course, and while publishers had a good idea which books would probably do well and which would not, it was impossible to know if they had a hit on their hands. Although they were all factors in the mix, no one thing or even combination of things—favorable reviews, publicity, advertising, an attractive cover, good distribution in bookstores—guaranteed that a book would sell significantly better than others. Two related factors did seem to matter, however: quality and word-of-mouth. Bestsellers were usually well written and, at least as important, readers recommended them to other readers, these the key ingredients to getting on the exalted *New York Times* list. Authors usually blamed their publisher for not doing anything and everything possible to making their book a bestseller, but it was more likely that the work was simply not the stuff of water cooler or lunch-with-the-ladies talk.[9]

In hot pursuit of a bestselling book or at least one that would kick off a solid literary career, aspiring authors continued to flock to the center of the American publishing world, New York City. Once there, more determined writers were apt to find a full-time job too demanding on a number of levels, and promptly joined the legion of those who came before them by becoming cab drivers as a means of support. Driving a cab was one of the few ways in which artists of all kinds could make a decent living and still find time to write. Recent college graduates dreaming of having their first novel published were "hacking" a few days a week and writing the remaining days, taking advantage of the chronic shortage of drivers in the city. Not only could one choose which days and hours to work but one could make $20 in a ten-hour shift, pretty good money in the early 1960s (about $160 in today's dollars, when the rent for a small apartment in the East Village did not require one to be an investment banker). Writers also liked the detachment that came with the job, finding that they did have to invest any of their emotional energy in driving people around the city. Writing ad copy was always an option for someone with a modicum of talent, but that would drain the creativity from one's own work, many felt. Picking up some great dialogue was a nice side benefit of driving a cab, with even a Hemingway unable to make up some of the things riders said in the backseat.[10]

New York's hold on writers paralleled the postwar triumph of the city as the global capital of many industries. Unlike in England, where London remained the only city where a serious writer had to be at least part of the time, there were in fact viable alternatives to New York City for American authors. Chicago, San Francisco, and Boston all remained respectable literary communities, and many writers were scattered throughout the South. Many if not most dedicated writers believed New York was the only city for them, however, as it presented the greatest chance of recognition. Just being in New York conveyed a kind of commitment to the trade; with some notable exceptions, a vague suspicion surrounded most writers choosing to live in other places, as if they might be dabbling amateurs versus true professionals. As between the wars, the major publishers and literary agents were based in New York, as were the leading publications that reviewed books. If nothing else, the city's cocktail party circuit was heavily populated by key figures from the literary scene, making it wise for writers wanting to be noticed to make the social rounds.[11]

While the literary elite devoted to the craft of writing hesitated to venture anywhere west of the Hudson, the nexus of Hollywood was home for the new superstars in the field. "The literary world is awakening to the fact that a small group of authors ... are reaching shiny, new, professional horizons," reported Richard Schickel in *Life* magazine in 1964, these lucky few novelists "getting wondrously rich." Everything about the Los Angeles literary scene, if one could even call it that, was different than the one in New York. Rather than slowly accumulating wealth after publishing numerous books over the course of a decades-long career—the usual path of a successful author—for example, this small literary clique in Southern California was making big money virtually overnight. Given the rewards to be had, the formula for this brand of cinematic fiction was surprisingly simple: choose a popular topic, take a fact-like approach, include lots of sex, and provide a happy ending. Had Hollywood cracked the bestseller code, writers back East must have wondered?[12]

In these wildly popular novels (sometimes referred to as "nonfiction fiction") by authors such as Harold Robbins and Irving Wallace, charismatic protagonists, either heroes or villains, found themselves somehow involved in a corporate power struggle, all the while jetting off to some exotic location and embarking on a series of romantic encounters. Some kind of crisis that threatened to destroy the world was another standard story line, with our leading man or woman finding true love by the book's final page to readers' great delight. The hardcover, paperback, and movie rights to this kind of literary property, which was often sold simply on the basis of an outline or even a conversation between author and publisher, could make $1 million or more. Robbins, Wallace, and a handful of other writers like James Michener and Herman Wouk who had made large sums of money through film rights had come to be known as "movelists," a dubious distinction among serious authors but one that almost guaranteed a sizable bank account.[13]

The emergence of "movelists" in the early 1960s was no doubt a thorn in the side of writers who had pounded out books for years to find themselves not only not rich but considered yesterday's news. For writers who had been around for some time, it was the near impossibility of staying at the top of the game for very long that proved most frustrating. As always, an older writer's longevity or body of work mattered little, as publishers, reviewers, and readers turned their attention to younger ones with fresh ideas and different takes on life. Even after enjoying great fame, a writer could be quickly forgotten, considered past his or her prime. William Saroyan certainly felt that way, telling his personal story when he was fifty-five years old. Saroyan had won the Pulitzer Prize for Drama in 1940 for his *The Time of Your Life* and an Academy Award for Best Story in 1943 for the film *The Human Comedy*, and he continued to pour out high-quality plays, books, and short stories for the next quarter-century. By 1964, however, Saroyan was well out of favor among critics, making him feel that his substantial contributions to the literary world were now of little value. Saroyan had outlasted many other well-known writers, but endurance was insignificant in an industry where the new and different tended to be most rewarded.[14]

We Must Speak Our Minds

Like many authors, Saroyan had strong political leanings that only rarely came into public view. (He was almost court martialed during World War II for writing what was deemed to be a "pacifist" novel, and he turned down the Pulitzer Prize he had won on the grounds that art and commerce should not mix.) Since the late 1930s, in fact, the literary landscape of the United States had been remarkably politics-free, reflecting a conscious awareness that aligning oneself with any ideological cause or side would be bad for business. The same could not be said to be true of the Nobel Prize for Literature, however. An element of politics appeared to be a factor in awarding the prize to all of the

Chapter 3 • The Intellectuals, 1960–1979

six Americans who had won it by 1965. The respective winning works by Sinclair Lewis, Eugene O'Neill, Pearl Buck, William Faulkner, Ernest Hemingway, and John Steinbeck were all in some way critiques of the American way of life, something the Swedish judges (Stockholm academics) apparently considered to be prize-winning material.[15]

Beginning around 1960, however, writers had shown more interest in political matters, although more related to specific issues than as sweeping partisanship. The election of JFK that year had much to do with this, of course; his political platform and charisma seemed to wake up many Americans who had drowsed through the postwar era. Through the early sixties, the civil rights movement had also stirred up Americans' interest in political affairs, especially that among writers who were in a position to let their stance on the issue be known and to try to persuade others to think similarly. By 1965, however, it was clearly the Vietnam War that had become the most politicized issue among writers (and arguably the general public), with the vast majority opposing intervention by the United States in Southeast Asia. Robert Lowell and Arthur Miller had each turned down invitations to the White House as a means of protesting LBJ's policies toward Vietnam, and Saul Bellow had recently sponsored a demonstration for peace in Washington. "We feel that the present course of the Johnson Administration in Vietnam is intolerable and that we must speak our minds," wrote author and editor Irving Howe in the *New York Times*, feeling that when it came to this particular issue, "the writer can't keep to his attic."[16]

Howe was one of many American writers who felt they could no longer keep to their attics when it came to Vietnam. In 1966, Howe, Alfred Kazin, and twenty-two other prominent writers held a press conference to demand an immediate cessation of the bombing of North Vietnam and for the Johnson Administration to reach a negotiated settlement to end the war. The writers also managed to hold a private meeting with Vice President Hubert Humphrey, who they felt had abandoned his liberal and humanitarian ways to support the President on Vietnam. The military's increasing commitment to the "undeclared" war would only lead to disaster, the group told the American people and the Vice-President, a prophecy that turned out to be correct.[17]

While political activism among American writers definitely

skewed left, conservatives did occasionally join the fray. Two years after that protest of United States involvement in the Vietnam War, no less than 220 writers and members of the Authors Guild of America signed a petition of support for the nation's intervention. William F. Buckley Jr., the editor of the *National Review*, and Frank S. Meyer, the magazine's book review editor, sent the petition, which urged that the country remain committed to the war until it reached "an honorable conclusion," to President Johnson and President-elect Nixon. Interestingly, John Dos Passos, who had gone to the Soviet Union to study socialism in the late 1920s and had taken part in the communism-oriented First American Writers Congress in 1935, was among the signers of the petition.[18]

As it became increasingly clear that a countercultural movement was crystalizing in the mid-sixties, critics made note of the new kind of politicized American writer. With no shortage of problems everywhere one looked during these turbulent times (poverty, racism, and crime, to name just a few), American writers were assigned and took on the weighty role of trying to make sense of the troubled country and world. Mirroring LBJ's Great Society domestic programs designed to help those in need (and, a generation earlier, FDR's Works Progress Administration programs), writers used their skills to produce what *Saturday Review* called "sagas of the underprivileged."[19] More broadly, both nonfiction and fiction were becoming more sociological in scope, addressing some of the key issues of the day.[20]

As writers and their work became more socially relevant, Americans took the literary community more seriously, and afforded them an unprecedented degree of status. The Kennedy Administration's commitment to the arts lingered, and the rising number of young people getting a college education also contributed to this greater respect for the American writer. Writers' new authority, grounded in their role as cultural arbiters, could be seen in the marketplace for new work. Publishers were bidding against each other to land the next Joseph Heller or James Baldwin, eager to find a writer with a unique and hopefully acerbic take on some aspect of American life. With their black humor, comic novels were all the rage at the time in part because they made social criticism funny, an appealing aspect of any novel.[21]

Through the late sixties and into the seventies, American writers

Chapter 3 • The Intellectuals, 1960–1979

of all political persuasions fought on behalf of writers in other countries who were being treated unfairly by oppressive governments. In 1968, for example, 500 American writers signed a petition requesting that the Soviet government grant amnesty to two Russian writers who had been in jail for two years. Western intellectuals including Hannah Arendt, Daniel Bell, and William F. Buckley had for some time sought the release of the writers who had been convicted on grounds of having published material that was critical of the Soviet regime, with this appeal the most concerted effort to free the men.[22] The Soviet's treatment of Aleksandr Solzhenitsyn made headlines in the United States, with fellow writers among the loudest voices of protest. The 1970 Nobel Prize-winning author (whose books were banned in Russia) was continually harassed and not permitted to use research institutions in his homeland, a means of punishing the man for his critical views on Soviet policies. Saul Bellow and Arthur Schlesinger, who each seemed to be at the forefront of actions to defend writers' rights, were part of a committee formed in 1972 to pressure the Soviets to allow Solzhenitsyn to continue his important work.[23]

American writers were especially interested in the plight of Soviet and Polish Jews. In 1967, twenty-two American writers, including six Pulitzer Prize winners, appealed to writers in the Soviet Union to do whatever they could to preserve Jewish cultural life in that country. There were 3 million Jews in the Soviet Union, but severe restrictions were placed on their ability to engage in any form of Jewish culture. Robert Penn Warren, Ralph Ellison, Archibald MacLeish, Arthur Miller and others signed the letter that was sent to the Soviet group of writers who were about to meet at a conference in Moscow.[24] Two years later, a group led by Saul Bellow and Irving Howe asked the Soviet Writers Union to help stem the anti–Semitism that had intensified in Russia since its support of the Arabs in the most recent Middle East conflict.[25] Also in 1969, a contingent of American writers (including "Yip" Harburg, the lyricist most famous perhaps for writing the words to all the songs in *The Wizard of Oz*) protested the upsurge of anti–Semitism in Poland that was being encouraged by some leaders of that country's government. Most of Poland's 25,000 Jews had applied for exit visas, as clear a sign as any of the persecution they were experiencing.[26]

Although the kind of activism that helped define the counterculture had largely faded by the late 1970s, American writers continued to speak up when they saw injustice. President Carter's concerted interested in human rights for people of other nations was additional impetus for American authors to publically support foreign writers who they felt were being mistreated by their respective governments. Even before Carter took office, he frequently espoused freedoms for dissidents, a political platform that resonated with writers such as Arthur Miller, Edward Albee, Kurt Vonnegut, and Allen Ginsberg. In January 1977, for example, those members of the American Center of P.E.N. (Poets, Essayists, Editors and Novelists) sent a message to the President-elect, protesting the ways in which Vaclav Havel and other Czech writers were being bullied and jailed by the government in Prague. Members of another writers' organization, The Authors League of America, felt similarly, with John Hersey, Ralph Ellison, Arthur Schlesinger, and William Styron among the individuals to send a letter of protest to President Gustav Husak of Czechoslovakia.[27] Freedom of speech should be a basic right for all people, these American writers felt, following in the footsteps of the Founding Fathers who had composed some pretty good works themselves.

The Slum of Journalism

While some of the nation's best and brightest fought for social justice when not writing important, critically-acclaimed books, other writers scratched out a living by freelancing. Freelancing was an attractive alternative to those journalists who were averse to the various constraints that came with a staff position at a newspaper or magazine. Freelancing offered writers the freedom to choose projects as they wished, liberating them from a nine to five job that bound them to a desk and to an editor who doled out assignments as he or she wished. (The term derived from for-hire knights who used their lances for whoever happened to need their castle defended.) Freelancers typically pitched article ideas to editors, giving them a greater sense of creative control than when told what to write. Freelancing was ideally suited to self-motivated writers who were able to ride the highs and lows that came with unsteady work.[28]

Chapter 3 • The Intellectuals, 1960–1979

While many freelancers found the job well suited to their lifestyle and temperament, there were of course challenges. The lack of boundaries between one's professional and personal lives could be a problem even for the more adaptable; it was difficult to turn off one's brain at 5 p.m. and over weekends, and the possibility of always working could make one feel guilty when one elected to take some time to relax. The feast or famine nature of freelancing could also be demanding; working 18 hours a day one week and zero hours the next took some getting used to. The need to constantly come up with new article ideas also was not easy, and a source of pressure for individuals who might have thought their well of creativity would never run dry. And more so than a relatively cushy staff job, speed was of the essence, as the faster one wrote the faster one could move on to another gig.[29]

Perhaps the greatest challenge, however, was the dwindling opportunities for writers wanting to be a hired gun. Many of the "slick" magazines that welcomed freelance material and paid well for it, e.g., *Collier's*, *Woman's Home Companion*, and *Coronet*, were now out of business. The golden age of magazine freelancing that between the world wars served as the financial bread and butter for so many writers (even published authors) was no more. The top of the heap for freelancers, the *Saturday Evening Post*, had by the late 1960s hired staff writers, as had most of the more popular magazines of the day. With these changes, the reputation of freelancers fell, the job now perceived as belonging to journalists who lacked the talent to get a full-time position at a magazine or newspaper.[30]

As distressing as those journalists wanting to go solo were the financial prospects of freelancing. Magazines didn't pay freelancers what they used to, making it difficult for them to make a good living even if they were lucky enough to regularly get assignments. The *New York Times Magazine* was in 1967 paying $400 for a major article, *Harper's* and *Atlantic Monthly* anywhere from $250 to $750, *Esquire* $1,000, *Playboy*, *Ladies Home Journal*, *McCall's* and *Holiday* around $2,000, and *LIFE* anywhere from $2,500 to $5,000. The average freelancer might pick up a couple of such major features and a few other smaller projects a year, providing an annual income of perhaps $5,000 ($35,000 in today's money). More problematic was the fact that magazines were known to reject articles after they were written, making the freelancer's hard work mostly for naught (he or she might receive a "kill fee" of about $150). An editor having second thoughts about a particular piece or leaving his or her job after commissioning an article were other risks freelancers had to face.[31]

While freelancers had their freedom, there were other, more psychological costs. An obsession with the mailbox was not unusual, with some freelancers known to keep one eye on their typewriter and one out their window to see if the mailman was arriving. Great anticipation surrounded forthcoming letters of acceptance or rejection for article ideas submitted to editors, making freelancers very familiar with the schedule of their local postman. Some freelancers, unable to wait a few more minutes, would walk down their street to meet the mailman before he got to their house, while others would call the post office to make sure a particular letter was not sitting in the undeliverable box for some reason. Still others would check to see if a letter they were expecting was at a neighbor's house, no doubt adding to their already well-established image as the slightly loony writer living down the block.[32]

Their odd relationship with their mailbox notwithstanding, versatility was one of the primary attributes of a successful freelancer. Virtually any kind of writing was considered fair game among freelancers able to switch gears at a moment's notice. In addition to writing a wide range of magazine pieces, freelancers might very well write captions for photos and illustrations, publicity releases, reviews of all sorts, and material for both radio and television. Collaborating with an author on a book was also not unusual, but not the most pleasant of tasks given the fair chance of clashing styles and differences of opinion. The frenetic nature of the freelancing profession was often reflected by his or her workspace. Ideas were frequently tacked up on the walls, and piles of unfinished (and likely never to be finished) work seemed to be everywhere. Old magazines and long overdue library books might also be strewn about, as well as newspaper clippings and typewriter ribbons dating back to the Eisenhower Administration.[33]

A familiarity with certain tricks also went into the makings of a good freelancer. The art of expanding sentences was essential for projects that paid by the word. ("Freelance writer" could be rewritten as "writer who freelances," for example, a simple change that earned 50 percent more money.) Even assignments that did not pay by the word

Chapter 3 • The Intellectuals, 1960–1979

could be more lucrative if they had a lot of them. More text meant that editors would not have to shell out money for artwork to fill space, making heft a definite plus. Freelancers also knew how to play their cards when presenting article ideas to editors. Pitching just one was a bad idea, they quickly learned, as the editor was likely to reject it based purely on principle. Pitching a large number of ideas, say a dozen, was also a mistake, as the editor would be so overwhelmed he would likely reject all of them. Three, however, was considered just right, as it was a quantity that the editor could process, and still afforded him or her the opportunity to reject a majority of ideas while still approving one.[34]

While freelancers were very aware that time was money, it was common for them to procrastinate, an extension of their relative freedom. Staff writers went to an office everyday, but freelancers usually worked at home, where many distractions enticed them to put off that assignment for which they had signed up. Some of this procrastination was actually strategic; turning something in close to the expected publication date gave the editor less time to demand a rewrite. Considerable planning went into handing in a piece at the last minute possible. Rather than mail it in, which took an unknown number of days, those able personally delivered it to their anxious editor. (E-mail was still a quarter-century away.) Some freelancers who lived in New York City or its suburbs finished the piece on a portable typewriter on a subway or train, cutting it extremely close. Those cutting it too close had to literally think fast; commuters might see a now frenzied freelancer furiously typing away in a corner of Penn Station, wondering who this literary vagabond was and what important thing was he or she working on.[35]

Despite all of his or her determination and tricks, things got only tougher for the freelance writer through the seventies. "For most freelancers," *Time* observed in 1978, "magazine writing today has become the slum of journalism—overcrowded, underpaid, and littered with rejection slips." There had been 25,000 freelancers in the United States at the peak of the profession between the wars, a Marquette University professor estimated, but now there were only about 300 individuals making a living at it. Paradoxically, the magazine industry was thriving; advertising revenue was at an all time, and the number of titles had grown to 9,200. The problem was that too many writers were pursuing a limited number of assignments, allowing editors to pay the same fees they had for decades while inflation had galloped. *National Geographic* and *Reader's Digest* now paid the most for a major article ($4,500 and $3,000, respectively), but most freelancers would have been more than happy to grab the $900 *Better Homes and Gardens* or $875 *TV Guide* was offering.[36]

Can I Have One?

Despite the rough going for freelancers, the generally good times for publishing showed no signs of slowing down in the late sixties. The book business became a $2 billion industry in 1966, an all-time high that made Wall Street investors take a close look at publishing companies that were publically traded. Some had predicted that Americans would stop reading books as television technology and the shows themselves improved. That wasn't the case, however; Americans seemed more interested than ever in reading books and in the people who wrote them. The success of the business was all the more remarkable given how little it had actually changed over the course of the last century. The industry had gotten much bigger, of course, but the workings remained essentially the same. Publishers received manuscripts from writers or agents, and edited, printed, and packaged a select few; these were then distributed to and sold in bookstores and promoted via the media of the times. Change of any significance to this tried and true system was resisted, with precious little innovation taking place in the industry since the Civil War. From this perspective, it was perhaps amazing that the book business had not gone the way of the horse and buggy or petticoat.[37]

The growth of the publishing industry and respect for writers encouraged more young people to consider going into the profession. Novelists were frequently invited to speak and meet with students at college campuses, a perfect opportunity for the latter to ask the former if pursuing a literary career would be a wise decision. Students were no doubt shocked when an author gave them an emphatic "no," expecting a successful writer to thoroughly endorse the idea. Authors were inclined to be totally honest by informing the literary minded that writing was a very tough way to make a living, and that they should consider

Chapter 3 • The Intellectuals, 1960–1979

other career options unless they had a trust fund at their disposal. Students were then known to counter by naming a handful of writers—Saul Bellow, Katherine Anne Porter, Mary McCarthy, and Truman Capote were popular choices—who had not only produced great work but made a lot of money doing so. While authors made it clear that these were rare exceptions (and that a fair number of now rich writers had many lean years waiting for their ship to come in), they were usually not successful in persuading students with books on the brain to swap their typewriters for slide rules or briefcases.[38]

Young people convinced that they would not only change the world through their writing but make wads of cash at it would have been surprised to learn how many people would expect them to give books away for free. Authors were constantly asked for complimentary copies, thinking that their friend, colleague, or complete stranger they just met had an unlimited supply of them stacked up somewhere in his or her house. Contrary to popular belief, this was not at all true. Publishers a half century ago, just like today, gave a dozen or so copies to authors, with most of those typically passed off to reviewers or journalists who could help publicize the book. One was often kept for the bookshelf, and mom and dad might get another, but there was no large cache in the closet. Besides that, what incentive was there for an author to give out free copies when his or her source of income relied on people buying them?[39]

Perhaps working under the alternative assumption that authors might have a printing press in their basements to produce copies on demand, the range of individuals asking, "Can I have one?" was truly remarkable: classmates and teachers from high school who one hadn't heard from in twenty years; the plumber or electrician noticing that the book on the coffee table bears one's name; letter writers intrigued by the subject but claiming that they could not afford to purchase a copy; neighbors who saw it on display at the local bookstore, but owned more televisions than books; relatives who requested one not just for themselves at Christmastime but a copy they could send to each member of the extended family. Librarians too sometimes pushed for a handout despite obviously having a budget to purchase new books. "Why don't you donate a few copies to the library?" they kindly asked authors, once in a while even having the nerve to add, "Then we can use our money for more important books." Authors often had to buy copies from the publisher (at a discount) to meet the demand for free books, a peculiar and frustrating situation.[40]

Fortunately, a good number of people were willing to part with a few dollars to buy books. Helping to drive the book business in the late 1960s was a dynamic fiction market. In the two decades since the end of the war, three generations of novelists were said to have appeared on the literary scene, offering readers a smorgasbord of fictional work. Writers such as Norman Mailer, Gore Vidal, and James Jones were part of the first group; LeRoi Jones, Philip Roth, Susan Sontag, John Updike, and John Barth were key figures of the second; and Jerome Charyn, Joyce Carol Oates, Heather Ross Miller, and William Melvin Kelley were representative of the third. While the second generation was "thoroughly disorganized," according to Richard Kostelanetz, editor of *The Young American Writers*, the third was "more thoroughly educated and culturally sophisticated than earlier chronological sets," meaning this new group was more skilled in certain respects. If there was one theme among contemporary novelists, it was "discontinuity of experience," he noted, with some of this intentional non-linear style lost on both readers and critics.[41]

Indeed, not everyone was impressed with the fancy techniques of the youngest generation of American writers. There was too much style and not enough substance, some felt, the art of writing coming off as more important than the story. For some critics, like John Leonard, the book reviewer for the *New York Times*, too few writers were producing "radical" fiction, meaning novels that put forth highly charged (and well-written) political opinions. There was no shortage of "autobiographical debauches in which the omnipresent 'I' pretends to be synonymous with authenticity, as though craft were a trick instead of a method of organizing one's perceptions," he proposed, but not many novels that had anything meaningful to say.[42]

Love Story

The showy kind of fiction being published was perhaps an attempt by writers to become darlings in the media as the literary world

Chapter 3 • The Intellectuals, 1960–1979

increasingly crossed paths with show business. In the past, more fortunate writers had a choice in terms of retaining their creative freedom or making money, but those two goals often did not intersect. Fitzgerald and Faulkner, for example, were able to do each by writing the books they wanted to and using the movies as a means of generating large amounts of cash. (The playwright Clifford Odets, on the other hand, was acknowledged as having completely "sold out," using his considerable talent to write or direct any Hollywood screenplay if it would pay for things like a giant pool in his backyard.) Arthur Miller's 1956 marriage to Marilyn Monroe served to bridge the distance between "high" and "low" culture, however, bringing the rarified air of literature closer to that of entertainment and paving the way for a new kind of celebrity author.[43]

Writers' higher profile in show business in the 1960s and 1970s could be seen across American popular culture. The literary elite could be legitimately considered superstars of their day, with their personal lives often covered by the media. A-list authors were even invited on *The Tonight Show* in order to provide witty banter for a mass audience. Hip magazines like *Playboy* and *Esquire* began featuring short stories and literary interviews, and even *Vogue* and *Harper's Bazaar* included the occasional poem and book review. These were clear indications that writers in America had crossed over a kind of tipping point; they still might be rather odd ducks, but now they were seen as valuable members of society plagued with problems to be solved. Intelligence had become cool, one might say, a turn of events that authors were more than happy to exploit.[44]

Erich Segal was perhaps the best example of this cross-pollination between intellectualism and mass culture. An associate professor of classics at Yale, Segal began drifting into the popular realm in the 1960s, writing pop songs, screenplays, and books for musicals. On Valentine's Day 1970, Segal's weepy *Love Story* was published; the novel was a monster hit (it was the bestselling work of fiction that year), and was immediately green lit for a movie that was released in December. (The film became the highest grossing film of 1970.) Amazingly, Segal did not quit his day job at Yale, claiming that pursuing serious work by teaching the classics remained important to him. While he became somewhat of a laughing stock among intellectuals after innumerable interviews to shamelessly promote *Love Story* and the movie version ("the first printing of *Love Story* in paperback was the largest single printing of any book since the invention of movable type," he claimed in one of them),[45] his success was evident of the more blurry lines between the high and low. Susan Sontag and Norman Mailer had also crossed over in their own respective ways ("Mailer the celebrity has tended to overshadow Mailer the artist," *Nation* noted in 1977),[46] proving that it was indeed possible for brainy writers to realize great fame if they (or their agents) knew how to package their assets.[47]

As the cult of celebrity grew in the early 1970s, the quality of fiction appeared to slide even further. As in the decade after World War II, the novel was said to be in a state of decline, with various theories proposed regarding why. Pop psychology and sociology had infiltrated fiction, some argued, bringing a touchy-feely sensibility to the art form. Others believed that New Journalism—the style of news writing that co-opted certain literary techniques—had stolen the thunder of the novel. Blamed for a host of social ills, television was the culprit, still others claimed, with reading fiction too laborious compared to the passivity of the Boob Tube. Critics were hopeful there would be a turnaround as there was in the late fifties, however, as a bevy of new books by some top authors including Iris Murdoch, Doris Lessing, Peter De Vries, John Cheever, Bernard Malamud, James Jones, Kurt Vonnegut, and Philip Roth (the latter fittingly titled *The Great American Novel*) were published in the spring of 1973.[48]

Part of the problem could have been related to the gender politics that were playing out at the time. Perhaps as a backlash to the escalating feminist movement, gender identity, specifically masculinity, was proving to be an important element within writing culture in the 1970s. There was a "cult of masculinity" in American fiction, *Esquire* posited in 1972,[49] with *Saturday Review* suggesting that same year that contemporary novels contained a "masculine wilderness."[50] Beyond the work itself, gender discrimination in the industry was routine; editors and publishers at the time were still overwhelmingly men, male authors dominated most literary genres, and there was a certain macho-ness attached to the field as a whole. But men had always had the upper hand in literature in the United States, and some of the country's greatest work was undeniably masculine (virtually the entire oeuvre of

Hemingway, notably), making one question that gender dynamics were the primary problem in fiction.

As John Leonard had suggested a few years earlier, it was current novelists' skill with words, ironically, that was hurting fiction, according to other critics. "It seems to me that quite a few American authors are suffering from what I would call literary affluence," noted Anatole Broyard in 1974, thinking these writers were "so comfortably provided with talent and/or technique that they frequently indulge in conspicuous waste." Had writing somehow become too easy for those with a gift for the art, with apathy setting in among those not challenged by the mechanics of constructing sentences? The same could not be said of many of the great writers of earlier generations, Broyard felt, with no nonchalance or insouciance to be found in the works of such authors as Dos Passos, Steinbeck, and Erskine Caldwell.[51]

While critics parsed the universe of fiction to figure out why there weren't enough great novels being published, others were more concerned with how the publishing industry as a whole operated. Few could contend that there was a great divide within the writing community, where some were making fortunes and others were struggling to put food on the table. Going (much) further, some suggested there was a "literary mafia" in America that, like the criminal institution, wielded a great deal of unofficial power. Such an underground organization controlled the publishing business, some truly believed, with the spoils to be had doled out to a limited few. Not only those who felt they were excluded from the big money and fame subscribed to the idea. Truman Capote, who had made millions over the course of his career and was famous as any American writer, held there was indeed a literary mafia (specifically a Jewish one), and it was this group of people who were responsible for his lack of critical acceptance.[52]

Those who had yet to achieve success were more likely to make the case that the deck was stacked against most writers, however. Certain (and, yes, predominantly Jewish) figures at magazines such as the *New York Review*, *Commentary*, and *Dissent* exerted a tremendous degree of influence, the conspiracy theory went, with their editorial control extending to other magazines, the *New York Times*, and to the larger publishing and media worlds. Keeping out new voices who threatened the bottom-line of the established literary industry was the aim of this particular mafia, a less nefarious one compared to the Cosa Nostra yet a sinister presence to writers finding it impossible to be heard. A buddy system was at work in the literary mob, according to believers, with the "dons" determining which books got reviewed and what kind of books got published. Some thought the claim absurd—if anything, new writers often received more attention than long established ones—but there was no doubt that the gap between the winners and losers in the business was a very wide one.[53]

A Wonderful Exposition of Life

Even some of the biggest winners in the history of American writing had personal demons, of course, with large quantities of alcohol often used to try to exorcise them. Other countries had their fair share of literary drunks, but writing and drinking were almost synonymous in twentieth century America. Booze "has come to seem a natural accompaniment of the literary life," wrote Alfred Kazin in *Commentary* in 1976, a symbol of the profession's "loneliness, creative aspirations, and frenzies." It was often not discussed, but a look back at the relationship between writing and drinking in the United States beginning with Edgar Allan Poe was not at all pretty. (Much less attention was paid to writers' frequent habit of smoking, although tobacco might very well have killed more of them than did alcohol.) Sinclair Lewis, Eugene O'Neill, and William Faulkner (who together comprised a full half of the six Americans who had won the Nobel Prize in fiction up to that point) were either alcoholics or compulsive drinkers for much of their lives, and both Hemingway and Steinbeck each hit the bottle hard. The list seemed to go on and on. Fitzgerald and Ring Lardner were alcoholics (and each died in their forties), as were Jack London and John Berryman (each a suicide). Hart Crane had a drinking problem (and killed himself), as did J.P. Marquand, Wallace Stevens, E.E. Cummings, and Edna St. Vincent Millay. Some writers, including London, Dorothy Parker, and Dashiell Hammett wrote about their respective drinking problems, while most did not.[54]

What led so many writers to drink, and drink excessively? It was

Chapter 3 • The Intellectuals, 1960–1979

"the drive for success of every kind," Kazin proposed, "the hunger for prestige, fame, and money" in conjunction with "the burden put upon the creative self."[55] One psychiatrist actually did a study to try to figure out why so many great American writers drank like fish. Donald W. Goodwin of Washington University argued that there could be a genetic link between writing ability and alcoholism, with manic-depression perhaps the common thread. Fitzgerald, who was the poster child for the image of the imbibed author (he called alcohol the "writer's vice" and was known to introduce himself as "F. Scott Fitzgerald, the well-known alcoholic"), appeared to suffer from the condition. There were any number of other possible reasons for the close relationship between writing and drinking, however, including the need to bring out exhibitionism, increase sociability, encourage fantasy, bolster self-confidence, ease loneliness, or, most simply, relax after a long day of hard concentration.[56]

Writers' affinity for alcoholic beverages contributed to the all-too-common perception that they were prone towards going insane or somehow disappeared off the face of the Earth. It was true that many novelists who had considerable success with their first published book were never again heard from in the literary scene, a puzzling situation. The simplest explanation for this was that the writer said what he or she wanted to say in that book, and had made the wise decision not to keep repeating that basic idea in subsequent novels (something that occurred with surprising frequency). "Their incentive to write was to objectify the theme of their lives," as Mark Harris described such novelists' motivation, "to come to terms with the outer world [and] to solve certain problems of existence." Once having done that, these writers went off to do other things in their lives, but their brief literary career served as a source of bewilderment to critics' and readers' expectations for them to keep on producing books. With a popular novel under one's belt, one would have to be crazy to opt out of the profession, they concluded, a wrong and unfair presumption.[57]

Some of American writers' copious drinking also might have been due to not being acknowledged as among the best of their class. Judges for the Pulitzer Prize had an especially poor record when it came to recognizing great writers. Hemingway was a great example; he didn't win the award until 1953, a full twenty-seven years after his *The Sun*

Also Rises was published in 1926. Similarly, Faulkner didn't win until 1955, twenty-six years after his *The Sound and the Fury* was published in 1929. Ellen Glasgow didn't win until her twenty-third (and final) novel, and Upton Sinclair until his forty-seventh book. Erskine Caldwell was another great writer who had never received a Pulitzer Prize or, for that matter, a National Book Award. The author of such classics as *Tobacco Road*, *God's Little Acre*, and *North of the Danube*, Caldwell was for a time the best selling novelist in the world. Like Glasgow and Faulkner, however, Caldwell was a Southerner, something that lessened his chances of winning a major prize due a Northern bias among award committees.[58]

Prize committees' habit of ignoring great writers and great books for years or even decades could be seen as an inability to fully appreciate work in its own time. Even novelists themselves were inclined to think that most of the work being published at a given time was not very good, and that the field as a whole was not what it used to be. James Michener, whose books included *Tales of the South Pacific*, *Hawaii*, and *Centennial*, felt that fiction was playing a diminishing role in the life of the nation, a trend that had begun in the early twentieth century. The appearance of new amusements had offered Americans more ways to spend their leisure time, a process that was vastly accelerated by television. Interestingly, Michener, one of the world's most popular writers, actually felt that television was a superior medium than literature in certain genres, such as romance and crime. (Of the latter, *Kojak* and *Baretta* were particularly good, he thought.) However, while television was more vivid, there was no substitute for the personal experience that novels could offer, he added, naming Bernard Malamud, Saul Bellow, Joyce Carol Oates, and Joan Didion as contemporary authors whose books could and did change people's lives. Novels remained "a wonderful exposition of life," Michener continued to believe, uniquely able to offer social commentary in an increasingly complex world.[59]

Offering social commentary within the nonfiction arena was another matter, at least according to Lewis H. Lapham. Lapham had in 1977 recently become the editor of *Harper's*, and was frustrated by how few American writers made good contributors to the magazine. Only a handful of writers were knowledgeable about a particular subject and had the ability to present a clear argument, he felt, making it difficult to find people who could engage in public discourse and join the "national conversation." There was no shortage of theory-laden academics, opinionated social critics, and investigative journalists, but their poor writing skills or personal biases disqualified them as possible contributors. Lapham was not surprisingly a big fan of the magazine essay, believing forty pages was more than enough space for a writer to make his or her case. Ninety-five percent of nonfiction books were "puffed-up" articles, he argued, but publishers needed a product that ran into hundreds of pages to justify charging the current retail price of about $10.[60]

Numero Uno

Just when the world of literature could have used something big to happen to break out from its malaise, along came the television mini-series *Roots*. *Roots*, an eight-part, twelve-hour show that aired in January 1977, was based on Alex Haley's novel published the previous year. The novel (subtitled *The Saga of an American Family*) turned the American Dream upside down with its window into African American culture from slavery to the present day, exposing the nation's tragic record of racism. Haley's own story was a fascinating one. After collaborating with Malcolm X on his autobiography, Haley embarked on a genealogical journey, tracing his family's roots to his African ancestor who was sold into slavery. Haley's heavily researched story, embellished to make it a work of fiction for a popular audience, was in the right place at the right time. "No other novelist or historian has provided such a shattering, human view of slavery," wrote Jason Berry in his review of the novel for *The Nation*, convinced that Haley had captured something important within the mid–1970s zeitgeist. No novel since William Styron's (much criticized) 1967 *The Confessions of Nat Turner* had brought such public attention to the country's shameful legacy of slavery and, arguably, made a bigger splash in American literature.[61]

While the novel had already become a number one bestseller when it was published in 1976, the miniseries interpretation of *Roots* became nothing short of a cultural phenomenon. The Nielsen ratings for the show went through the roof; the finale remains today the third most watched television show of all time in the United States. The last extremely popular televisual treatment of a novel had been Irwin Shaw's *Rich Man, Poor Man,* but even that did not come close to the buzz that surrounded *Roots.* James Michener, who was becoming as much of a cultural critic as a novelist in the late 1970s, felt that the television serialization of *Roots* was not just a media phenomenon but a very important event for American writers and publishers. From one respect, he pointed out, the show served as a twelve-hour advertisement for a novel, with many viewers immediately heading to their local bookstore to buy the $12.50 hardcover edition (the paperback had yet to be released). "It is this century's *Uncle Tom's Cabin*," he said of *Roots,* and "the black man's answer to *Gone With the Wind*."[62]

While Michener was delighted that many Americans, some perhaps who had never before entered a bookstore, were buying copies of *Roots,* he worried that publishers would try to repeat its aberrational success. Junior editors would be charged with the mission of finding a manuscript that could be sold to television even before it was published, he fretted, not just a likely futile task but also one that put the proverbial cart before the horse. Publishers should be in the book business first, Michener insisted, a stance that could be challenged due to the piles of money the television mini-series generated for Harcourt. The upside was that television producers would no doubt seek out other books that could be translated to their medium, raising the public profile of literature and hopefully increasing its popularity.[63]

While Haley had made millions from *Roots,* he was hardly the best selling American writer as the seventies drew to a close. Hugely popular authors such as Michener, Irving Wallace, and Leon Uris may have been giving him a run for his money, but it was Harold Robbins who held the envious title of number 1 novelist in the United States (and actually the world). The author of more than a dozen novels filled with the never boring lifestyles of rich and famous characters had come a very long way since his childhood as an orphan in Hell's Kitchen. (Robbins lived in Beverly Hills most of the year but summered in Cannes and wintered in Acapulco.) The man was not reluctant to flaunt his top position. "I'm Numero Uno," he told Herbert Mitgang of the *New*

Chapter 3 • The Intellectuals, 1960–1979

York Times in 1978, seeing himself as the literary equivalent to the champ of his respective field, Muhammad Ali. Robbins contributed hard work to his amazing success, claiming he could write for thirty consecutive hours when his creative juices were flowing. Rather than employ the typical novelistic device of plot, Robbins used a social issue or industry as the platform for his books, another reason why he stood out from the crowd. Most of his books were turned into movies (by Harold Robbins International, his own production company), adding to his staggering wealth. Robbins had yet to win any major literary prizes, however, a distinction he cared little about. "Every day 30,000 people in 50 different countries keep me in style by buying a Harold Robbins novel," he crowed, the eight million books he sold every year the only prize that really mattered.[64]

While Robbins headed to the south of France in summer, many New York-based writers also escaped the heat and humidity by going to pleasanter surroundings for the season. Where better-known writers spent their summers was a defining element of literary culture (at least to other writers) in the late 1970s, something that continues to this day. If they were able to get out of town for an extended period, New York-based writers tended to summer in one of three places: Cape Cod in Massachusetts, its neighboring islands Martha's Vineyard and Nantucket, or the Hamptons on Long Island. Famous figures of the literary set including Eugene O'Neill, John Cheever, Edmund Wilson and Alfred Knopf had long headed to Cape Cod, especially its outer towns of Truro, Wellfleet, and Provincetown. Cape Cod was (and is) decidedly low-key, with the writing crowd there likely to eschew work in favor of swimming, gardening, clamming, or playing tennis. On the Vineyard, however, writers like Art Buchwald and Lillian Hellman were known to get together to discuss works in progress, making it a kind of literary colony.[65] MacDowell, near Peterborough, New Hampshire, and Yaddo, at Saratoga Springs, New York, remained the ultimate literary colonies, however; each was famous for decades for their monastery-like peace and quiet that suited writers seeking minimal distraction.[66]

The Hamptons and its nearby towns also had a long history for the writing crowd. Sara and Gerald Murphy, who served as the prototypes for Nicole and Dick Diver in Fitzgerald's *Tender is the Night*, had owned a beach house there, and John Steinbeck was a visible figure in

Sag Harbor for decades. The Hamptons but were quite different in tone than reserved Cape Cod and Martha's Vineyard, however. Then as now, there was an active party scene in the Hamptons, with any number of writers, editors, and publishers likely to show up at one fabulous fete after another. Truman Capote, Joseph Heller, and George Plimpton were just a few of the guests in attendance at one such party thrown for John Updike in the summer of 1977, and Edward Albee's annual bash at his spread in Montauk was one of the places for the rich and famous to see and be seen. When not partying at night, however, writers summering in the Hamptons were likely to be hard at work in the day, more interested in their next book deal than looking for mollusks on the beach. The sheer beauty and special light, as well as its proximity to Manhattan, drew writers and artists to the Hamptons like moths to a flame, something that hasn't changed much despite its seemingly never ending upscaling.[67] Both deal-making and the pursuit of pleasure would reach new heights in the following decades, altering the course of the American writer once again.

CHAPTER 4

The Individualists, 1980–1999

"One writes because there's no help for it, because one doesn't really have a choice in the matter."
—Arthur Krystal, 1997

In 1997, Ian Hamilton reflected on the transformation of the American writer over the past three decades. Hamilton, a British author, recalled visiting the United States for the first time in the late sixties, finding it to be a place of intense energy, especially for writers who thrived on living on the edge. "The best American writers, it was widely and admiringly believed in the 60's, were crazy, drunk or dead by their own hands," he wrote in the *New York Times*, the country at the peak of the counterculture somewhere one would "either cheer up or crack up." Now, however, America was a land of "killjoys," Hamilton observed, all of its exuberance and fun crushed by a cultural mandate for sense and sensibility. "Nobody drinks, nobody smokes, nobody even thinks of going mad," he continued, this self-control extending to writers' now placatory relationships with their editor or publisher. "They are now expected to project themselves as cool, well-organized achievers," Hamilton wistfully described contemporary American writers, deeming them to be "just like everybody else."[1]

As Hamilton's musings suggest, the 1980s and 1990s were a period of tremendous change for the American writer. Neo-conservatism and the triumph of consumer capitalism had a big impact on the literary community during these two decades, making the image of the radical writer operating on the fringes of society even more the stuff of mythology. The United States became a much more fragmented place over this period, something that also helped to redefine and, more specifically, individualize the American writer. Like the reigning academic theory of postmodernism, literary culture seemed to no longer have a central core or grand narrative, instead playing out through the dynamic forces of pluralism and self-expression. As well, more attention than ever before was given to the creative experience, an exploration that shed additional light on the psychological makeup of individuals who had decided to make writing their calling in life.

Writers in Residence

The altered landscape of the American writer had much to do with major changes taking place in the publishing business, specifically the devaluation of the short story. Once the primary way for writers to make money, the short story had by 1980 become a much more specialized literary form compared to its heyday decades earlier. Only a few general interest magazines such as *The New Yorker, Redbook, The Atlantic,* and *Esquire* included short stories, and book publishers almost ignored them because they did not sell well. If writing novels or freelancing were financially dubious, the short story market was positively disastrous. It's fair to say that no one could now make a living as a full-time short story writer, as its audience was just too small. Defenders of the short story argued that it more closely resembled real life than the novel, however; our lives were actually a series of different vignettes versus one long, linear saga. A minor revival of the short story was underway, in fact, as a new generation of writers adopted it as their literary genre of choice because of its manageable size, both to read and write. Fewer people were reading short stories but more people were writing them, just another paradox in the strange universe of literary culture.[2]

The literary underground was another genre whose popularity had greatly dwindled by the 1980s. Since the nineteenth century, the image of the American writer as an outsider was firmly entrenched in the popular imagination, an impression that the Beats had magnified in the late fifties. Avant-garde writers opposing the status quo were thus once not just the stuff of myth; success in the marketplace and bourgeoisie values really were rejected by a certain segment of writers in the 1950s and 1960s. One could even argue that the subversive artist working furiously in a tenement was the model for writers in the postwar years, despite the fact that many of them decided to "sell out" when corporations and the government came calling with job offers that actually paid money. That changed in the 1970s when the idealism of the counterculture faded, and the conservative swing in the 1980s only accelerated the demise of an influential literary underground.[3]

One thing that had not changed was New York's status as the epicenter of literary life. As always, however, communities of writers could be found all over the country. Some were settling in Montana for its solitude, scenic beauty, and low cost of living. Livingston and Missoula were two towns in that state where more writers were putting down roots and, when not working on a novel, short story, or poem, probably taking advantage of the best fly-fishing in the nation. A few other recognized authors were living in remote regions of the vast state, finding it the perfect place for not just catching trout but for the kind of contemplation they needed to produce their best work.[4]

One place new Montanans were coming from was San Francisco, which had a much more vibrant literary scene, but also allowed writers to pursue their own respective paths without having to face much social pressure. Although San Francisco had a very rich literary tradition and the echoes from the counterculture could still be felt, there was no getting around the fact that it, like every other city in America, was cast in the shadow of New York. "San Francisco is not the right spot for those concerned with making it," noted resident author Herbert Gold, feeling those with major ambition had to head east if they wanted to become stars in the field.[5]

Another place to find talented writers seeking to avoid the angst of New York in the early eighties was Key West. A half-century after Hemingway decided to stay for a while on the island (he ended up living there for a decade, during which he produced almost half of his life's work), authors had actually become somewhat of a tourist attraction in the Florida town. The local library even published a pamphlet called "Writers in Residence" to help visitors spot one of the fifty-five or so notable authors residing there. Tennessee Williams, John Dos Passos, Robert Frost, and Hart Crane had also dwelled in Key West for part of their lives, giving the place a rich literary history that drew other writers. Travel agencies were packaging writing workshops and seminars (many of them held in the Tennessee Williams Fine Arts Center) for the bookish, making some compare the town to Paris in the 1920s. While that was a big stretch, Key West was indeed a place filled with interesting characters and where one could have a very good time—two things that writers were known to greatly appreciate. Unlike in the Hamptons, another top spot for writers, talk of agents, advances, deals, options, and contracts was discouraged, a refreshing climate for those more interested in the work than the money.[6]

Even some die-hard Manhattanites were finding sanctuary in the New York City borough to their east. Brooklyn may have been more formally known as the borough of churches, but anyone at all literary-minded knew it as the borough of writers. While still urban, Brooklyn offered a more comfortable alternative to perpetually frenzied Manhattan, making it not surprising that so many writers past and present called it home. Whether it was the energy of its working class, the cultural clash of its neighborhoods, or the education to be gained in its streets, Brooklyn was a special place that seeded the imaginations of author after author since Walt Whitman. Proximity to a plethora of politically minded people who tended to talk very fast no doubt paid off big dividends in terms of storytelling. If nothing else, the enduring, in-scale architectural style of the borough, vastness of Prospect Park, and of course the grandeur of the Brooklyn Bridge gave that part of New York City a powerful and authentic sense of place that seemed to help inform the work that was produced there. Brooklyn felt like a collection of small towns to its residents, a good environment for writers to collect and compose their thoughts (before taking the subway to meet their agent or editor in Manhattan). Beyond its sheer profusion of life, being close to the action but not in the midst of it relieved some of the pressures that came with a literary life, this perhaps accounting for why it remained a place that many writers chose to live and work.[7]

Postwritum Depression

Regardless of where American writers set up shop, youth was becoming a greater asset to possess. The standard narrative of a notable author's professional life tended to trace the struggles in the early part of his or her career, after which the writer experienced a successful breakthrough followed by a long series of mostly critically acclaimed books. What was usually left out of the story was the diminishing emotional returns that such a writer was likely to realize as he or she got older and published more books. For a writer (and maybe anyone in any other profession), nothing could match the excitement of youthful ambition, and the initial satisfaction that came from being recognized for one's work. Over time, having conquered the worlds one had sought, a kind of complacency often set in, with no achievement able to generate the thrill of one's younger (and tougher) days. Not helping matters was that it became increasingly difficult to come up with new themes and techniques, as by now writers had settled into a familiar pattern designed more for efficiency than innovation. Writers who had become famous were perhaps most vulnerable to this phenomenon, as heaps of praise and other, non-literary opportunities diverted them from their work.[8]

Whether old or young, it took confidence and courage to write, many agreed, as one was exposing oneself to criticism as soon as others read the material. Young writers, however, were particularly vulnerable to critics' reviews; a too vitriolic assessment of one's work at an early age could very well make him or her think twice about pursuing a literary career. Editors too could be cruel when rejecting submissions from new or veteran writers, so much so that it made some stop working for months. Showing work in progress to friends or fellow writers could also be tricky as any and all opinions were of course subjective. Some authors refused to show unpublished material to anyone except their editor, while others eagerly circulated chapters or entire manuscripts to get feedback while there was time to make revisions. Still others (including Joan Didion and her husband and fellow writer John Gregory Dunne) shared drafts only with their spouses, those being the only people whom they could trust with offering an honest opinion.[9]

Meeting one's own critical standards could be even tougher than meeting those of others. While writing could be as simple as turning on a faucet and seeing the water pour out, it was more often acknowledged as being a difficult and painful process. Sometimes the sentences would just not appear, a puzzling and frustrating experience for anyone who wrote for a living. Agents sometimes would have to cajole writers who were falling behind schedule on a book with a financial incentive, exchanging money for pages. Changing one' writing environment was a typical attempt to get the juices flowing, whether that be relocating to a different city, country, or continent or simply rearranging the furniture in one's room. If that didn't work, procrastination of one sort or another typically took hold, with virtually anything considered more enjoyable than trying to write. Not knowing where a story should go, the loneliness of sitting in a room by oneself, or one's expectations for what a work could and should be were all reasons for writers to freeze up, whether it be for a few days or a decade or two.[10]

Freezing up could also result from a negative review, especially if it was in the widely read, highly respected *New York Times*. Authors were known to remember one bad review from many years ago but forget dozens of good ones, an indication of the degree to which negative criticism was seared in their memory. "Book reviews generate far more passion than sex does in the literary world," proposed Thomas Fleming of that newspaper in 1985, the subject perhaps the last remaining taboo in the industry. Authors were reluctant to complain about a bad review with people they did not know well, recognizing it would sound like sour grapes. But with their good friends, spouses, and shrinks, authors were not at all reluctant to share their thoughts, most of them inevitably about how the reviewer got it so wrong.[11]

Even great writers, including some of the most famous ones, were bothered by bad reviews, with more than a few finding that they could not work for days after reading one. This was surprising, not only because one would think the views of any single individual didn't matter much in the big scheme of things, but also given that most reviews were written by part-timers who were just taking a break from their real jobs. Magazine and newspaper editors often chose professors, journalists, or politicians to review books because they were considered experts in a particular subject. Reviewers who were professional writers

Chapter 4 • The Individualists, 1980–1999

were frequently especially cruel to other writers, a reflection of their general antipathy towards those in the same field. Reviews did not have to be entirely negative to get an author's goat. Even one critical sentence in a long, positive review could spoil the whole thing, making one wonder why authors chose to read them in the first place.[12]

Writers' sensitivity to any kind of criticism was a reflection of their general inability to detach themselves from their work. Joyce Carol Oates considered writers to be "the world's worst critics," at least when it came to their own material. Famous characters of the literary past—Chaucer, Thomas Hardy, Franz Kafka, and Chekhov, to name just a few—were all unduly tough on themselves, suggesting that a heavy dose of self-criticism was woven into the DNA of a writer. (Overinflated egos could be seen as a kind of psychic cover-up for this insecurity.) Writers were known to experience a kind of paralysis as they lost faith in their own abilities and considered themselves basically talentless, something reinforced if professional critics agreed with that assessment. Even the best of writers had little idea of the relative merit of any particular work of their own; it wasn't unusual for one to think highly of a book that critics hated, and vice-versa. While working on a book, however, writers were inclined to think it was the best thing he or she had ever done, a mental trick perhaps to simply get it done.[13]

Because so much time and energy often went into writing a book, a wide range of emotions could be associated with its completion. "Completing a book can be an exhilarating, draining, even traumatic experience for a writer," noted Charles Salzberg in 1987, "a time of fantastic hope and tremendous doubt." Because there was no real definable moment or measure for when a book was finished—more material could always be added and existing material endlessly rewritten—an author had to choose some subjectively determined point to consider it done. (Writing was somewhat like parenting in that no matter how much effort one put into each activity, there was a nagging feeling that one could have done more.) A novelist's pace frequently picked up when nearing completion, whether that was due to the winnowing of options for the characters in the story or, more practically, an increased desire to be through with it. A sense of elation and excitement over how the book would be received usually followed, and sometimes the feeling that there would be no point in starting another because it would be difficult to outdo oneself.[14]

Soon after the high of sending off a manuscript to an editor, however, a low could very well set in. Many novelists found that they missed the characters they had gotten to know so well, a testament to these writers' vivid imaginations. Others felt at sea after finishing something that had so occupied them for so long, not knowing exactly what they should be doing. Catching up on life was the healthiest option, but doing long neglected home repairs or going fishing could hardly compete with the euphoria that came with finishing a book. Unchanneled energy could be a problem for certain writers, with some destructive habits picked up to fill the void. Mania or, conversely, what Salzberg called "postwritum depression" might kick in among the more emotionally involved, each of these states derailing the afflicted writer for a period of time. But after a couple of months or perhaps a year, most writers were back in business, ready to start the whole process all over again.[15]

The Writer's Disease

Most writers just starting out could only wish they could one day experience the emotional rollercoaster ride that followed sending off a manuscript that would soon be published. Those planning on a literary career dreamed of publishers in bidding wars for one's work, glowing reviews in the *New York Times,* and even perhaps being recognized by strangers on the street for being "that writer." Something much different was likely in store for the overwhelming majority of novices, however, with very few ways to prepare oneself for what would almost certainly be a rocky path. Writing classes in college might have taught the mechanics of the trade, but only the school of hard knocks offered instruction in how one was likely to be treated by the rather cruel publishing industry. One institution in Manhattan called Writer's Prep, however, was dedicated to bridging the gap between young writers' expectations and more probable realities. Writer's Prep's curriculum covered just four subjects—indifference, rejection, misunderstanding, and humiliation—exactly what the average writer would by all odds face in large doses in the years ahead.[16]

Chapter 4 • The Individualists, 1980–1999

Some schooling in learning how not to be jealous or envious of other writers could have been useful. Envy was "the writer's disease," according to Bonita Friedman of the *New York Times*, a vocational hazard that made its victims despise hearing about a fellow author's or journalist's triumph. Success by a writer who was younger than oneself was especially disturbing, as it was evidence that the upstart was ahead in the literary game. Hearing that a perceived rival scored a sweet victory—getting a favorable review, winning a book prize, or landing a piece in *The New Yorker*, say—could very well bring out the green-eyed beast, even among elite writers. (The recipient of a major prize was subject to considerable contempt by colleagues, while coming in second would earn much sympathy.) All kinds of psychological reasons could be read into why people, especially writers, became envious, but for many the only escape from it was diving into one's work. There one could find sanctuary from what Friedman called a "scorpion of the mind," as even the seemingly miraculous success of others could not thwart the sway of one's muse when it was in good form.[17]

The strong streak of envy among many writers was just one barrier to them being friends with one another. Writers were infamous for not being friends with other writers, deeming anyone in the same profession to be a critic—something that simply came with the occupation. Writers had best beware of choosing another writer as a chum, standard thinking in the field went, as down deep he or she could not help but wish for failure for that so-called friend. As well, good writers saved their real passion for their work, it was said, making them unable to devote much emotional energy to a relationship. Whether or not they wanted to, writers considered friendships as raw material, not a very good foundation by which to establish a meaningful connection to another human being. Writers often fantasized about being friends with a writer whose work they admired, but common wisdom suggested that the association would be doomed from the start, a casualty of the inherent competitiveness and jealousy of the job. Writers' keen perceptive skills were also detrimental to creating a genuine bond with a colleague, as that kind of scrutiny would reveal too many flaws on the part of each respective party for a mutually respectful acquaintance to take develop.[18]

Linda Bamber, a professor of English at Tufts University, disagreed that amity between writers was futile, however. "Writers can be friends," she insisted, the prevailing view a result of clashes and feuds among famous authors simply being more news-friendly than everyday harmonious relationships. While admittedly risky, literary friendships were likely to be intense and rewarding, she felt, as two interesting minds formed an intellectual and creative alliance. Because of the nature of the profession, writers tended to be lonely people much of the time, making it actually quite sensible for two or more of them to congregate in some way. Support and understanding from a person in the same boat went a long way, some writers reported, and the ideas were likely to fly assuming there was mutual agreement that discussing work was fair territory.[19]

Support and understanding from a fellow writer were likely to be much needed in the early 1990s. The paths of the publishing business and the American economy as a whole continued to run parallel, not a good thing for either during the most recent recession. The boom times of the 1980s were clearly over, making publishers in many cases regret the huge advances they had paid to big-name authors whose books did not make money. Major publishers had engaged in bidding wars and paid millions of dollars in advances to authors whose books they mistakenly believed would become instant bestsellers. The publishing industry had swelled to $13 billion in 1990 but was in a big slump, quite a reversal of fortune from the wild ride of the 1980s. Before the October 1987 stock market crash, some agents had become almost as famous as their clients for their ability to land giant advances, and once-loyal authors were jumping from publisher to publisher if there was more money to be made. Even first-time authors had been awarded contracts in the hundreds of thousands of dollars, another decision that proved to be unwise in the age of excess. Now in the red, publishers were laying off employees, and showing considerably more fiscal restraint in all aspects of the business.[20]

In financial trouble, publishers pressed more notable authors to go out on the road to hawk their books. Signings at bookstores had always been a good way to move copies in bulk, and publishers capitalized on authors' celebrity status by urging them to make public appearances when they had a new release. Even quite famous authors such as Bill Cosby who didn't need the money typically did book tours

Chapter 4 • The Individualists, 1980–1999

as it afforded them the opportunity to meet with thousands of people and enhance their high profile. Selling a hundred copies at an event would generate a few hundred dollars in royalties, certainly not enough to justify the time and effort for wealthy celebrities. Combined with a few media appearances, however, a book tour offered authors a great deal of publicity tailored to a local market and, not incidentally, the chance to receive heaping quantities of praise and adulation, reason enough to endure the ordeal.[21]

Appearances at bookstores were hardly easy, especially when it came to signing copies of books for readers. Every person wanting to meet an author was of course different, making it necessary for authors to have dozens or perhaps hundreds of personalized mini-conversations with complete strangers. Some readers were happy to just get their book signed and move on, but others seized the opportunity to enjoy their brief moment with an author whom they liked or adored. Readers who wanted the author to inscribe a personal message in the book were the most demanding. (I would ask authors to write "Dear Larry: Thanks for the idea." Most agreed to my admittedly obnoxious request.) Some authors understandably refused to write any inscriptions, as they received the same royalty per book regardless of whether they did or did not. Others (like the Welsh thriller writer Ken Follett) agreed to sign only hardcover copies, as the royalty rate was lower on paperbacks, a rather greedy policy considering the piles of money he was making not just from his scads of bestsellers but also from the movie rights to them as well.[22]

All the book signings in the world, however, could not rescue the publishing business from the mess it had gotten into. Beyond its lingering financial troubles, new work being published seemed scattered, with no recognizable guiding school or philosophy. American fiction was "in a muddle," thought Sven Birkets in 1992, more concerned with the genre as a whole than with individual works. Writers just weren't sure what kind of novel to be writing and readers didn't know what kind of novel they should be reading, according to Birkets, this accounting for the mushiness of the genre. Such a complaint was hardly new, of course. Since the 1960s, the demise of the American novel had been widely proclaimed—an assertion that proved to be wrong given how much excellent work had been created over the past few decades.[23]

Still, the possibility that there was a major problem in American fiction was being taken seriously, especially after Tom Wolfe's 1990 controversial essay in *Harper's*. In his "Stalking the Billion-Footed Beast: A Literary Manifesto for the New Social Novel," the famous author in the white suit accused his colleagues of focusing on themselves in their work rather than the harsh realities of the world, leaving journalists to that dirty but more relevant job. Wolfe had used the nineteenth century social novel as a model for his 1987 bestseller *The Bonfire of the Vanities*, and he urged his contemporaries to take a similar approach to extricate fiction out of the minutia of writers' personal experience or vision.[24] Not everyone agreed with Wolfe's assessment, however. "It's true that social realism hasn't been the hallmark of American fiction for the past 40 years, but, as been proven time and again, strict realism is not the one true path to greatness in the novel," argued Nicolas Lemann in *Washington Monthly*. "Novelists should be judged on the basis of their skill as novelists, not as reporters," Lemann concluded, citing Faulkner as a superb American writer who had little interest in applying a kind of journalistic approach to fiction.[25]

A More Pluralistic Society

Part of the problem in American fiction could have been due to the publishing business's obsession with youth. Since the mid–1980s, publishers had eagerly pursued the work of young writers, so much so that a kind of literary "Brat Pack" was said to have taken up residence within the industry. (The reference was of course to the group of young actors who often populated 1980s movies about teenage angst.) Twenty-year olds were landing high-powered agents, trying to follow in the footsteps of other writers still in college but having their novels published. The youth movement in American fiction had started in 1984 with the publication of Jay McInerney's *Bright Lights, Big City*. Soon after the success of that novel, a parade of "new voices" appeared, notably Bret Easton Ellis with his also bestselling *Less Than Zero*. Having made big money on those titles, a literary sub-genre was born, with dozens of works written by twenty-somethings published over the next few years. Critics questioned the writing abilities of these first-time novelists but gave generally kind reviews because of the alleged sociological significance of the books. Such authors were documenting the plight of disenfranchised youth in the materialistic 1980s, it was commonly held, earning them the esteemed title of "spokespeople for their generation." The second novels of these same authors typically flopped, but that was not a major concern for their publishers. Newer "new voices" had by then been discovered, good news in terms of recapturing readers' attention, at least for a short while.[26]

While publishers' focus on young writers was a shallow (but very profitable) marketing effort, their new interest in the work of people of color was a more legitimate, long-term enterprise. Multiculturalism had become a buzzword in many aspects of American life, and literature too became caught up in the aim to be more inclusive. "As America's view of what constitutes 'literature' expands to include the perspectives of a more pluralistic society, the publication of literary works by minorities is becoming increasingly encouraged," Lisa See Kendall observed in *Publishers Weekly* in 1990. Books about Native American culture by Native American authors had recently entered the mainstream, for example, a sign that "ethnic" literature could appeal to a broad audience of readers.[27] Fiction by American Hispanics was also getting more popular, especially after novelist Oscar Hijuelos won the 1990 Pulitzer Prize for *The Mambo Kings Play Songs of Love*.[28] With her *The Joy Luck Club*, Amy Tan had already put Asian Americans on the literary map, but new works by and about Chinese and Japanese Americans were being published that more realistically portrayed the racism those groups of citizens had faced and continued to confront.[29]

Within the multicultural space, however, publishers were most excited about the opportunity presented by African American authors. Beginning around 1990, there was a concerted effort by publishers to market books that would appeal to a historically ignored audience of readers. A "Black and Read" section was featured at the 1990 American Booksellers Association, for example, a clear attempt to show booksellers the wide range of books available by African American authors and illustrators.[30] Publishers tended to release books by African American authors around Black History Month (February), but that was gradually changing as they recognized there was a year-round market for books appealing to readers interested in African American culture.[31]

Quickly realizing that works by minorities represented much more than a niche market, publishers raised the stakes by offering huge advances to certain African American writers. In 1992, for example, Pocket Books paid $2.64 million for the reprint rights to Terry McMillan's *Waiting to Exhale*, a number that was second only to the $3 million paid in 1987 for those rights to Scott Turow's *Presumed Innocent*.[32] Soon after her windfall, McMillan, along with another extremely successful African American author and poet, Maya Angelou, endorsed an NEA initiative designed to start more creative writing programs at black colleges. None of the country's 117 historically black schools at the time offered a degree program in creative writing, amazingly enough, not a good thing if America's literary landscape was going to become more diverse. "It's important that young Black students know that it is possible to become a writer," McMillan said in support of the idea, making it clear that developing into an author like herself was not simply "something that happens to people who are chosen."[33]

Recognition of African American authors continued to escalate. In 1993, novelist Toni Morrison won the Nobel Prize for Literature, the first time in which the award was given to an African American (and the first time since 1962 that any American had won the prize). A former editor at Random House, Morrison taught creative writing at Princeton when not writing bestselling novels steeped in the African American experience. (Her *Beloved* had won the 1987 Pulitzer Prize for Fiction.[34]) Just weeks after Morrison won the Nobel Prize, Oprah Winfrey's production company optioned *Beloved*, the kicker being that Oprah herself was considering starring in the film version. (She did indeed appear in the movie.) Spike Lee's production company had recently acquired the film rights to Morrison's 1974 novel *Sula*, making the author quite the hot property in Hollywood.[35] More important than those headlines, perhaps, African Americans had become avid book buyers now that publishers had acknowledged there was a relatively untapped market. African Americans spent $178 million on books in 1993, according to Target Market News, with women, as usual, accounting for most of the sales.[36]

Chapter 4 • The Individualists, 1980–1999

By 1995, it was clear that books by African American authors were not a passing fad. "Swarms of books with commercial appeal by and about blacks are now stocked on shelves at [the bookstore chain] Dalton's," reported *Black Enterprise* that year, adding that about 80 titles with African American themes were being published annually. While some African American writers, notably Angelou, E. Lynn Harris, Walter Mosley, Nathan McCall, and Cornell West, were enjoying considerable success, there were few black employees at major publishers and few black literary agents, making some wonder if the industry had become as pluralistic as it might have appeared.[37] Still, there was no denying the fact that American literature had been irrevocably altered in a relatively short amount of time. Ralph Ellison's 1953 masterpiece, *The Invisible Man*, had documented the African American experience like no book before it, but now there was a growing body of literature dedicated to that same pursuit.[38]

Alone in a Crowd

Alongside the pluralization of American literature in the 1990s was a close examination of the process of writing itself. *Writer* magazine regularly featured articles by writers offering some kind of insight in the field, making it (much like *Bookman* in the 1920s and early 1930s and the *Saturday Review of Literature* in the postwar years) a central repository of the literary experience. One regular topic the magazine addressed was the simple nature of being a writer in a society that knew relatively little about the profession. Indeed, while many if not most Americans wanted to be authors, they rarely understood how writers actually did what they did. Where do you get your ideas? How long does it take to write a book? What if you get stuck in the middle? How do you know when you reached the end? Such common questions revealed that writing was considered a mysterious process, steeped in the enigmatic world of creativity.[39]

Writers were fully aware that the job they considered simply the way they made their living was often viewed as a baffling enterprise. Writers would look up to find people staring at them as they worked, the latter wondering perhaps if there should be more to the act than thinking hard and stringing words together. "Are you writing something?" a stranger might ask, begging the question of course what kind of material was he or she producing. Others might talk to a writer while he or she was working, not realizing that that would be a major distraction or thinking that writing didn't really count as serious work. Whispering or telling pests to be quiet often backfired, as it put pressure on the writer to "create" now that conditions were supposedly perfect.[40]

Much of the process of writing had to do with following a standard routine, contributor after contributor to *Writer* emphasized. Having a routine was the difference between success and failure, many writers reported, lending support to Woody Allen's famous adage that 80 percent of life was just showing up. It was not unusual for writers to admit they knew people who were smarter than they, had better stories to tell, and even possessed more literary talent, but the latter simply did not know how to put their skills to use. Over time, more accomplished writers developed certain habits to maximize their productivity, finding structure to enable creativity rather than deter it. Some writers were almost superstitious when preparing to work, the slightest alteration in their usual pattern of activity able to scare away their muse.[41]

Not surprisingly, the standard trope of writer-as-lone-wolf was a common theme among contributors to *Writer*. "Some loneliness, some separation, is at the heart of the writing process," stated Nancy Springer in 1993, going so far as to say that happy, well-adjusted people didn't write because they were not compelled to. Writers had their noses "pressed to the windows," Springer, an author of fantasy novels and books for children, maintained, a nice metaphor for their role as observers of versus participants in life.[42] Other writers, speaking for themselves and everyone else in the profession, said much the same thing. "The writer is neither in the world nor apart from it," proposed Judith Alguire that same year, "neither the dispassionate observer nor completely engaged." Alguire, an author of fiction, believed that most writers felt "alone in a crowd," something that was perfectly fine with them. Going further, Alguire argued that it was impossible for genuine writers to completely take part in whatever was currently taking place around them, as they could not fully free themselves from being

Chapter 4 • The Individualists, 1980–1999

observers of the action. As many had noted, she suggested that writers' first inclination was to extract material from their experiences, making them never entirely present in any situation. Unlike doctors, lawyers, or any other profession, writers were always writers, seeing themselves as characters in a story of their own design.[43]

This merging of a writer's personal and professional life was considered by some to be a unique thing in American culture. In fact, the often-heard phrase "the writing life" reflected the all-encompassing literary orientation of a writer, a concept that had no real equivalent in other occupations. (The only possible exception was sex workers who were sometimes said to live a "life of prostitution," and arguably shared a similar detachment from society because of their jobs.) The editor and critic Arthur Krystal argued that writing was a means of making sense of life, explaining perhaps why those who had committed themselves to it had difficulty establishing boundaries between working and not working. The fact that there was always potentially something else to write and that one could thus always be writing compounded this struggle to have a social life completely free from work.[44]

This inability for writers to separate themselves from their work could be a dangerous thing, many agreed. A kind of addictive quality might very well be attached to the profession. Mornings, writers were known to walk directly from their bed to their workspace, picking up from where they left off the previous night. When working on something requiring considerable intensity, days and nights tended to blur together, with little or no interaction with other people. For writers of fiction, the imaginary universe one chose to create could become all consuming, not a particularly healthy lifestyle. One could get used to the isolation, and just assume it was one of the many downsides of the business. Suddenly realizing that they hadn't had a face-to-face conversation with another human being for a few days and that take-out had become their primary form of subsistence, however, some writers tried to put limitations on their work, such as by committing to put down their pen or shut off their computer at a certain time of day. Unfortunately, these efforts often didn't work; the temptation to write was simply too great to do anything else despite the very sensible ground rules they had set.[45]

Even the hardest working writers, however, appreciated taking a break after completing a particular work. Allowing the soil to lay fallow for a period of time in order to regenerate itself was a good idea not only to keep sane but also to create a mental environment in which future material was likely to spring forth. Writers who had been around the block a few times were astutely aware that rest was good not just for one's body but for one's mind. A completely different change in scenery was the best way to refresh, a good number of writers felt, explaining why so many were drawn to communing with nature when not working. (Famous writers' getaways in the woods or near a beach were regular features in home and garden magazines.) Immersing oneself in the external world was a wonderful antidote to the pressures associated with the internal world of writing, one could say, the former allowing the literary part of one's brain to revitalize.[46]

Temporarily suspending writing in order to recharge one's literary batteries was entirely consistent with the growing recognition that the unconscious part of the human mind was responsible for much of our thinking. Writers frustrated that ideas for a work in progress were not coming quickly enough found that taking some time off ultimately led to greater productivity than trying to work harder and faster. A fundamental part of the creative process was, paradoxically, idleness: a means of allowing one's unconscious to work out solutions to problems on its own. Immersive activities in which one lost track of time, whether physical (swimming or hiking, say) or cognitive (painting or playing music, for example) were ideal for rejuvenating the analytical portion of the mind. Chores like vacuuming or washing a car were also kick starters for creativity, oddly enough, explaining why so many good ideas came to people when they were doing anything but trying to come with good ideas.[47] The best thing writers could do once in a while was not writing, recent neuroscience suggested, although that was a tall order for those with a deadline to meet or whose muse was ready to go.

The Noonday Devil

For those with a block, not writing was hardly a positive thing. While it no doubt existed, writer's block had not been a major issue within the literature dedicated to the field. As the writing process was closely scrutinized after the flourishing of the self-help movement and the rise of a therapy-oriented culture, however, the notion of a block became a primary concern. Writers hesitated to even mention "the b word," afraid that it (like impotence, perhaps) would become a self-fulfilling prophecy merely by acknowledging it was a possibility. ("Dry spell" was a bit better.) If asked, most writers claimed it had never happened to them but, in hushed tones, confessed that the dreaded affliction had struck someone they knew. Psychological theories for the condition abounded (fear of failure, fear of success, or an immobilizing degree of perfectionism, for example), but it was most likely that the writer was simply unclear about the direction his or her project should go. Before they began working everyday, writers were known to employ a variety of routines to ward off what was sometimes referred to as the "noonday devil." Hemingway reportedly sharpened twenty pencils as a ritual to discourage the onset of a block (and would stop in mid-sentence at the end of one day to make it easier to start writing the next), for example, and Willa Cather habitually read a passage from the Bible to court her own muse.[48]

What was perhaps cruelest about writer's block was its tendency to make a surprise attack on its victim. Writers would go through their normal routine and begin to work but, a couple of hours later, realize that there was nothing there, at least nothing one would ever want to share with another person. More coffee was needed, the writer might conclude, but, after two, three, four cups, still nothing. Panic could then set in, as the fear that one's literary tank was empty intensified. Moving to a new location was the next likely step, followed by a shifting of pen to mechanical device or vice versa. Eliminating those variables from the equation and still no results, writers were prone towards taking a break, whether that involved reading a newspaper, having a snack, or doing some jumping jacks to get the blood flowing. Virtually no method of breaking the spell was ruled out. More desperate, therapeutically informed writers were known to go out into the woods and scream as loud as they could, such a release able perhaps to purge the evil spirit from their literary soul.[49]

Fran Lebowitz, who had had considerable success with her two collections of essays, *Metropolitan Life* and *Social Studies*, had become the poster child of writer's block in the early nineties. After the latter was published in 1981, Lebowitz experienced a decade-long block, making her as famous for her "not writing" as her writing. Lebowitz had begun a novel but had completed just the first chapter by 1993, a remarkable lack of progress by any measure. "I am profoundly slothful," she candidly told *The Paris Review*, not something one was likely to hear from an author with a couple of hits. Interestingly, Lebowitz found not writing more demanding than writing; the former was psychically exhausting because one was expected to be doing the latter.[50] A small percentage of writers welcomed a block as it gave them permission to stop working and do other things. Seeing friends, going to the movies, watching television, or just catching up on sleep were rare delights for writers who normally put work in front of everything else. "The well's gone dry on me often enough that I recognize that one way to fill it is to relax and participate in life instead of agonizing because I think I have nothing to say," explained one such writer, making the most of her forced time off.[51]

Writers who had recovered from the noonday devil offered advice so others would not have to experience the condition. One possible solution was to jot down whatever one did over the past twenty-four hours simply to put one's brain into writing mode. Once in that state, the blockee could transition into more creative territory, a sensible way to ease the fear of the blank page.[52] Another way was to pretend to abandon the idea of writing a whole book. Knowing that there were two hundred or more pages to fill after writing the first one could be paralyzing, making it a useful trick to start with just one word or sentence. Such an approach was especially effective for novelists who were petrified by not knowing the direction their stories would go. Most novels were in fact not fully developed before the writer began work, reason enough to be content with starting small. From a little spark of an idea, kindling (characters, situations, locales) could be slowly added followed by heavier logs (plot twists), a more manageable way to tackle what was a monumental task.[53]

Like alcoholics, blocked writers often fell into the trap of promising themselves they would work "tomorrow," denying that they had a problem. When tomorrow came and no words appeared, however, they convinced themselves they were just not in the mood to write, also like alcoholics who would just not be in the mood to quit drinking. As those with any kind of addiction, confronting the problem head-on typically would not lead to a successful resolution. A more subtle approach to exorcise the literary demon was required, one which enabled the writer to free himself or herself from the loss of confidence that undergirded the inability to construct a sentence or paragraph. One good way was to eliminate any and all forms of self-criticism during the creative process. No idea was a bad idea if words appeared on paper, making it a good rule to not allow oneself to revise, correct, or edit a first draft when experiencing a block. Unlike doctors, writers did not have to get it right the first time, something the latter should keep in mind if the pressure was getting to them.[54]

Waiting to be inspired could also be a mistake for blocked writers. Inspiration was hardly a requirement for good writing, professionals knew, as telling a story simply and clearly was often good enough to be consistently published. Very little of life required one to be truly inspired or motivated in a special way, in fact, and writing was no exception. Experience was a far more valuable asset to possess than inspiration, experts pointed out, as one of the keys to a successful career resided not in creative genius but in the ability to produce work when one's muse was somewhere else. The notion of harnessing a mysterious force when it deigned to show up certainly added to the supposed glamour of writing, but it had little to do with the actually quite pedestrian nature of producing salable work and meeting deadlines.[55]

Writer to Reader, Reader to Writer

Taking a workmanlike approach to writing made extra sense when putting the job into a larger perspective. While writing was by definition a solitary act (even if one collaborated on a project), the oft-mentioned complaint of it being one of the loneliest of jobs might have been an exaggeration. Most writers chose both the time and place they worked, after all, while there were many other occupations, say an assembly line person in a factory, where one not only performed tasks by oneself but had little or no choice in the hours or the setting. Writing may not have been easy, but jotting down whatever happened to pop into one's head while sipping on delicious beverages in a pleasant café could hardly be considered hard labor. With all its challenges, writing still beat working, as the expression went, one reason no doubt why so many people sought to join the field's ranks.[56]

The simple fact that so many books had been written by so many people was more evidence that writing was not the horrible experience it was often said to be. For writers who had yet to be published, walking into a bookstore and seeing the thousands of books on the shelves could be a good or bad thing. A lot of so-so books seem to get published, one might conclude, bolstering an aspiring author's confidence. On the other hand, realizing that one's work would be part of such a large crowd, should one be lucky enough, tended to deflate the grandest of ambitions, and make one question if the whole thing was really worth all the time and effort. Constant rejection also made unpublished writers wonder if they would have been better off following all the advice they had been given to steer clear of a literary life. It was entirely typical for dozens of agents or editors to decline further interest in one's work after a query, a volley of negativity that did indeed discourage many of those starting out. More seasoned authors understood that lowering one's expectations would likely be in the best interests for average writers, as would comparing the odds of success in publishing to that of certain other fields. A baseball player getting a hit just one of three times would land him in that sport's Hall of Fame, for example, and it would be foolish for a poker player to expect to win every hand. "Losing," if one could call it that, should be seen as the normal state of affairs for most writers, veterans recognized, an idea that was likely strange for those eager to see their name of the spine of a book.[57]

With rejection and criticism so much a part of the literary experience, however, one had to wonder if writers had to have at least a streak of masochism in their genetic makeup to choose it as their profession. "Why does anyone consent to the emotional, financial, spiritual, and even physical contortions that are necessary in order to lead the writer's life in America today?" asked Kelley Cherry in *Writer*, fully aware that it couldn't be about the money. (Professional writers made an average $7,000 per year in 1993, according to the Authors Guild, an income level that put them well below the poverty line.[58]) Much

Chapter 4 • The Individualists, 1980–1999

patience was required to receive any form of external reward, in fact, as reviews and royalties typically came long after one had started writing a book. Rather, Cherry proposed that, despite all the reasons not to choose it as a career, writers were driven by a primal urge to tell people who they were. Readers necessarily had some sense of the identity of the writer whose work they chose to peruse, lending an existential dimension to the endeavor. Writing was thus a means of becoming more human, she posited, as good as any explanation for going down what was ordinarily a difficult path.[59]

Theory upon theory was put forth regarding the rationale for writers doing what they did. At its most basic level, some argued, writing was about someone sharing something with someone else, making connection a key component of the pursuit. The possibility that a book or perhaps just a single sentence or phrase could be deeply moving or at least interesting and informative to a reader was a prime motivation for writers to keep on writing. Through their work, writers had the potential of having a bond with far more people than they could in real life, a perspective that recast writing from its accepted view as a solitary and lonely exercise. "Writing links writer to reader, reader to writer, and reader to reader in a marvelous way," observed Melannie Svoboda in *America* in 1995, shifting the concept of the profession from an expression of individual creativity to a builder of relationships.[60]

Writers with the most profound takes on the art form were quick to challenge the notion that writing was a difficult if not agonizing act. For them, writing was a liberating force, and something that was instrumental in allowing them to, as the Army ad slogan went, be all they can be. Jane Yolen, for example, found writing to be a joyful experience, so much that a day without working left her feeling uncomfortable. Like actors, writers of fiction found themselves "inside" their characters, making the former miss the latter if they were not around them for some time. Writing could also serve as a therapeutic release, Yolen, a prolific author of books for children and teenagers, believed. "Authors get to parade their neuroses in public disguised as story," she explained, delighted to get paid for working out her hang-ups through her work instead of having to spend time and money on the couch of a shrink. "Writers get to treat their mental illnesses every day," Kurt Vonnegut had once said, like Yolen and no doubt many others finding their profession to be an ideal means of maintaining a sense of psychological wellbeing.[61]

It was Erica Jong, however, who offered what was perhaps the simplest and most compelling reason why writers wrote. "The truth is we write for love," she stated in 1997, only that able to counter the labor-intensity, skimpy financial rewards, and harsh criticism that came with the territory. Writers loved writing because if offered them the chance to say what they think, the author of *Fear of Flying* and a slew of other books believed, something even many rich people envied. Since she was a child, writing had made Jong feel "centered and whole," a gift that made it understandable why writers were happy to give their work away for such little compensation. "Do it for love and you cannot be stopped," Jong advised other writers, as powerful a rallying call for the profession as one could imagine.[62]

Damned by Dollars

Love of writing was very much a part of *Fear of Fifty*, a memoir Jong published in 1994. A near flood of memoirs by recognized authors appeared in the mid–1990s, in fact, appealing to bookish readers keen on peeking into the (often difficult) lives of writers they admired. William Styron's *Darkness Visible*, Susanna Kaysen's *Girl, Interrupted*, and Mary Karr's *The Liar's Club* were all part of this wave, with perhaps a couple of hundred such memoirs recently published. Autobiography was now hot, as writers seized the current interest in "confessionals" and revealed the skeletons in their respective closets. (Oprah culture and twelve-step programs had encouraged going public with what had once been a closely guarded personal life.) Some kind of dysfunction—alcoholism and mental illness were particularly popular—formed the backbone of this round of literary memoirs, with the once grammatically discouraged "I" usually telling the stories. "Our belief in the recuperative powers of letting it all hang out has never been stronger," wrote James Atlas for the *New York Times* in 1996, considering memoir-mania to be a prime example of "the triumph of the therapeutic."[63]

Chapter 4 • The Individualists, 1980-1999

Some kind of therapeutic release was just the thing for writers who felt that they did not receive the respect that people in other professions did. Since the 1920s, writers had rode a rollercoaster of public sentiment and, now with American society becoming ever more money-oriented, they were on a definite downslope. Mordecai Richler conceded that novelists like he were for the most part "a rude, disagreeable bunch," but blamed the way they were treated for their surliness. Complete strangers—mostly doctors and lawyers, it seemed—were not above asking him how much money he made on his last book, an odd and disturbing question given that no one would have the temerity to ask people in those professions what they had raked in on their last operation or legal case. These same people would also ask how many copies of that book were sold, this too rather rude since they were never quizzed about their respective job performances. While writers' social status was definitely higher than it had been decades earlier when declaring one wanted to be a novelist was tantamount to saying that one didn't really want to work for a living, the profession could still sometimes be seen as frivolous, especially during these days when one's annual income was so valued as a measure of an individual's worth.[64]

If there was any good news for writers at the end of the twentieth century, it was the introduction of a new technology offering an additional revenue stream: audiobooks. Authors had generally positive feelings about audiobooks, seeing them as another way their work could be enjoyed and purchased. Still, some valid questions had to be asked. Did literature lose something essential to the art form when translated into an audible medium, or was it perhaps enhanced? Should authors deliver their own material on audiobooks or should professional voice talent be used? Was editing a book to shorten its spoken length of time justifiable or was that a basic violation of the writer's creative intentions? Different authors answered such questions in different ways. Jimmy Carter was a big fan of the medium, pleased to have a few of his bestsellers put on audiotape. Carter likened the experience to listening to the radio when he was a child, an interesting point. The former President did his own recordings, finding it to be an enjoyable but challenging experience to speak the words he had written.[65]

John Gray was not surprisingly delighted to have his *Men Are from*

Mars, Women Are from Venus available as an audio version, as over a million copies of the tape had been sold. (His book was reportedly the most stolen tape from Barnes & Noble, but it still managed to be a bestseller for years.) Audiobooks were perfectly suited to Americans' busy lifestyles, he felt, allowing people to engage in a literary activity while traveling, working out, or doing other things. While Gray had had a huge hit, Stephen King was literally the king of audiobooks, having had more than three dozens of his works recorded. "You get a lot more out of [a book], I think, when you listen," he told *Publishers Weekly* in 1998, thinking it was a wonderful throwback to the days when literature was often read aloud as an evening pastime. Anne Rice, the popular author of vampire and supernatural novels, agreed. "I think Dickens would have loved the idea of audiobooks," she said, although he, like most authors, would likely not have preferred to have his masterpieces abridged to fit the length of a cassette tape.[66]

More than technology, however, it was money that was turning publishing into a much different industry as the century drew to a close. In the early 1980s, selling a few thousand copies of a book was enough for a major publisher to invite its author to write another. By the late 1990s, however, large publishers had raised their benchmark of success to a minimum of 25,000 hardcover copies, a difficult bar for most writers to meet. Conglomeration in the industry had pushed publishers to focus more on the bottom line, and in turn increased the pressure for writers to produce commercially profitable books. Over half of books sold in the United States were at price clubs like Sam's and Costco, a fact that encouraged the idea that literature had become just another consumer commodity. "Books and toilet paper are [now] viewed simply as different forms of trees," popular novelist Sara Paretsky told a group of booksellers at a trade convention in 1998, an unfortunate thing that writers were more than ever "damned by dollars."[67]

Although many Americans were ecstatic to see their annual income and net worth rise, the "gilded age" of the late nineties was not a pleasant time for most writers. Writers felt (and legitimately were) left out of the end of the century boom, and more than a bit jealous that many of the people they knew were getting rich. Many Wall Streeters and dot-commers were making millions while average writers

Chapter 4 • The Individualists, 1980–1999

struggled to sell their work, making the latter question their life's calling. Some writers, including virtually every author that was part of Oprah's Book Club, had hit paydirt, but these were rare exceptions. What was perhaps most frustrating for writers was that they believed (and perhaps really were) smarter than all their rich friends, magnifying the feeling that they had made a poor career choice. Should they have become lawyers or investment bankers like their friends? they wondered, resentful that they could not be part of the wild buying spree that was taking place all around them.[68]

In such a get-rich-quick environment, it was difficult not to think that writers were becoming obsolete, eclipsed by the mad rush for money. Would writers still be considered valuable members of society in a decade or two, some genuinely asked, as the making of money became the sole standard to judge a person's worth? Not helping matters was the prediction that books as we knew them would soon go away, replaced by a computer file. "Many of us still writing books today feel somewhat the way a blacksmith must have felt around 1920," observed nonfiction author Adam Hochschild a couple of months before the end of the century and millennium as the Internet revolutionized nearly every dimension of everyday life.[69] As the digital revolution unfolded, technology was indeed about to transform the literary universe, but opportunities impossible to be imagined lay in store for the American writer.

CHAPTER 5

The Nomads, 2000–

"We're living in a golden age for writers and writing."
—Stephen Marche, 2012

Like many writers in the very early part of the twenty-first century, Lynne Sharon Schwartz found herself increasingly distracted as she tried to work. There were now an almost infinite variety of diversions to be found online with one of them in particular—computer solitaire—so popular among her colleagues that Schwartz considered it "the writer's occupational disease." While causing no physical damage like many other addictions, there was little doubt that such online games did get in the way of getting work done, playing right into writers' (especially freelancers') habit to procrastinate for any reason at all. Five minutes of pre-work fun could very well lead to half an hour, and, after an hour or so of writing, the urge to play another game would often return. Hearts was another game that writers were particularly fond of, although those who wanted to really get away from it all preferred the trance inducing Tetris. "I was avoiding not only the blank screen but also all its ramifications," Schwartz confessed in the *New York Times*, disturbed by not just the usual challenges associated with writing but by the corporatization of publishing, decline of independent bookstores, and editors' annoying practice of not returning phone calls.[1]

The urge to play online games rather than write was just the tip of the iceberg in terms of the revolution that was taking place in publishing in the early 2000s. Stephen King himself admitted he was a "screen addict," proving that even highly productive writers had a problem logging off their computer.[2] Importantly, computers made it more possible to write anywhere and whenever one wanted, destabilizing the physical constraints of time and space. American writers increasingly were, as Mark Jacobson put it in 2000, "laptop nomads," working wherever they could find an electrical outlet (widespread Wi-Fi was still a few years away). "People typing away on laptop computers are in every Starbucks and coffee shop," Jacobson observed in *New York*, making one wonder who these writers were and what were they working on.[3]

At the turn of the twenty-first century, it was vividly clear that the Internet was changing much of everyday life in America and the world, with writing was no exception. Barriers to entry that had been in place since the modern publishing industry took shape a century earlier were tumbling down as writers wrestled away some of the power of publishers and agents. The Internet was allowing writers to literally connect with readers in a direct way that was impossible within the traditional model of publishing. Best of all, any writer could publish his or work online, cutting through the layers of levels that allowed just a select few to become authors. The musty, dusty world of publishing was finally changing, as technology empowered writers in a new, exciting way that the modernists, the realists, the intellectuals, and the individualists of the twentieth century could never have imagined.

Alongside the technological revolution, however, the usual challenges facing American writers have remained much the same. The writing process has continued to be parsed, and the qualities that define a writer heavily examined. Money is as big as a concern as ever for those choosing to be a writer, with a select few hitting the jackpot but the majority making significantly less than those in other professions. But new opportunities have undeniably opened up for writers determined and skilled enough to embrace the new model of publishing that has emerged over the past couple of decades. Long viewed by some as an endangered species, American writers beat on, as one of them put it almost a century ago, boats against the current.

A Rare Moment

Also like writers throughout the twentieth century, those of the early twenty-first were often the subject of what was typically viewed

The American Writer

as a puzzling creative process. Writers were frequently asked where their ideas came from, with their answers not at all clear. Ideas for books or stories could simmer for months or years or, conversely, be almost entirely formed in a matter of minutes. Ideas tended to surface all on their own—no one could say how or why—although it was entirely possible to consciously write a particular book or story, especially one of nonfiction. Writers of fiction were keenly aware that their livelihood rested on a mysterious course of events rooted in their unconscious. Stories seemed to summon novelists, their characters often appearing in dreams. Analyzing the story or trying to figure out why it called to them could make it disappear, making novelists steer clear of taking a rationale approach to the process. It was not unusual for novelists to lose their way in the middle of a book, finding that they were meticulously crafting the work rather than letting their imaginations run free. Putting the book down and working on something else for a while often allowed writers to get back on track, as the unconscious somehow figured out where the story should go.[4]

Because they freely admitted they did not have much control over their muse, many writers recognized that their unconscious played a big part in whatever they ultimately put down on paper. Writing was a way to vent one's unconscious, a Freudian might say, taking individuals on a voyage of self-discovery as distant memories came to the surface. Reading one's own work after some length of time suggested this was true. Where did these ideas come from? a writer might ask when proofing a manuscript months after composing a first draft, the material now almost unrecognizable. "Writing lifts me up and wafts me around in that sublime detachment from the here and now," Sherwin B. Nuland, the physician turned bestselling author poetically put it, finding what he called "the uncertain art" to be a perfect counterbalance to the precision and teamwork required for a surgeon like himself.[5]

Writers also confessed they were not beyond using tricks or gimmicks to woo their respective muse. Tacking some kind of inspirational message to the wall could act like a kind of talisman, some found, while others used a particular kind of music or even a specific song to attract creativity. (More unlucky writers found that they needed total silence to be productive, a difficult commodity to find. Some libraries had

Chapter 5 • The Nomads, 2000–

"quiet rooms," making those their workspace of choice; using earplugs was another option for the sound sensitive.) Other writers found that wearing certain clothes was conducive to getting the juices flowing, much like how an actor gained a greater sense of a role by literally dressing the part. Sue Grafton, the author of the extremely popular alphabet mysteries, put on a designer suit and carefully did her makeup and hair every morning, even if she was going to stay in a room all by herself for the entire day. Writing was a "real" job like any other, authors such as she felt, and looking like a professional was a means of doing one's best work. A lucky hat or lucky shirt was the thing for more superstitious writers, with others finding having an object of special sentimental value close by was needed to induce the goddess of art to stop by.[6]

For part-timers, transforming oneself into the writer within was a method unto its own. Those with children might not assume their writing identity until 8 or 9 p.m., meaning they had better maximize the little time they had to work. Given that this was the only part of the day not devoted to taking care of their family or keeping the house running, however, it was usually not much of a problem to get motivated to switch into writing mode. "The Superman inside you is emerging," freelance writer Jana Carvajal described this morphing process, finding herself "in a rare moment when no one and nothing needs your attention except the computer." Rather than dread or put off writing, as many full-timers did, people like Carvajal looked forward to the limited time they had to dwell in the imaginary worlds they created. Whether or not the material would be published and read by others was almost irrelevant; it was their love of writing itself that mattered most.[7]

Such a love of writing could often be detected at an early age, prime evidence that some people were simply born to pursue the craft. Dan Brown, whose *The Da Vinci Code* was a number one bestseller in 2003, "wrote" his first book when he was five years old by dictating the story to his mother who carefully jotted every word down. "I remember the excitement I felt to see my story expanding across sheet after sheet of white paper," Brown recalled, nothing short of thrilled to write his name at the bottom of the final page with a red crayon. Brown's mother then bound the pages of the story (titled *The Giraffe, the Pig, and the*

Pants on Fire) with yellow yarn and then created a book jacket out of a couple of pieces of cardboard, a beautiful thing that very likely further encouraged him to pursue a literary path. "Sadly, because of lack of demand, we never had to go back to press," Brown joked about his first book, taking considerable comfort in the fact that millions of copies of his latest one had been sold (and would soon be made into a movie starring Tom Hanks).[8]

As always, writers who had yet to reach the big time did what they could to pay the bills while they worked on their craft. The image of a newspaper reporter or advertising copywriter with a novel in progress stashed away in his or her desk was a popular one, but many aspiring authors knew that working with words for one's day job was best to be avoided. For decades, writers had driven cabs not just for the flexible hours that job afforded but also because it steered clear, so to speak, from the literary part of their brains. Teaching English or composition was tempting given the many positions to be found because of No Child Left Behind (the Act signed by President George Bush in 2002 that mandated states to set standards for teachers' qualifications and for students' aptitude in reading and math), but correcting essays and grading papers were known to sap most of a writer's creative energy. Although often physically draining, manual labor of one kind or another could provide a nice counterbalance to the more cerebral demands of writing. There should be no shame attached to cleaning houses, pumping gas, waiting tables, or washing dishes, many writers attested, as those kinds of jobs made few intrusions upon the imagination.[9]

Contemporary writers with day jobs could also take comfort in the fact that they were in some pretty good historic company. Eighteenth century British novelist Henry Fielding wrote his final work *Amelia* while serving as a government magistrate; nineteenth century British novelist Anthony Trollope produced a dozen or so books while working as a postal surveyor; Charlotte Bronte used her experiences as a governess for scenes in her *Jane Eyre*; Franz Kafka was inspired by his position as a legal secretary for the Workmen's Accident Insurance Institute in Czechoslovakia; T.S. Eliot was a clerk for Lloyd's Bank of London while writing *The Waste Land*; and William Faulkner produced some of his finest poetry when he wasn't sorting mail and delivering packages to students, faculty, and staff at the University of Mississippi.[10] For decades the poet Wallace Stevens worked at an insurance company, even choosing to keep the job after winning the Pulitzer Prize and being offered a teaching position at Harvard. Joseph Conrad had done some time in the Merchant Marines, a post that clearly provided valuable "life experience" for his work.[11] Interestingly, serving in the armed forces was a great job for a current part-time writer, those who had done it reported, as soldiers and sailors often had long stretches of time with absolutely nothing to do.[12]

While it was highly doubtful that most full-time writers would ever want to go back to moonlighting, part-timers found having a "real" job beneficial in various ways. Besides paying the bills, a nine-to-five job provided order and structure, something many writers needed. Without such a job, in other words, writers would feel too untethered, they explained, something that would actually make them less productive. Having a day job actually increased the efficiency of her writing, Sandra Hurtes reported in 2008, as it served as an anchor around which to schedule everything else. "And by replacing money worries and providing built-in boundaries, the muse can be freed," the freelance journalist added, perfectly happy with what she called her "double life." While many part-timers did not assume their writer identity until the evening, others found early in the morning to be the only opportunity for them to get some work done. For them, getting up at 5 a.m. to work for a couple of hours was not unusual, and a sign of how much they loved writing given that they were not doing it primarily for the money.[13]

While young people were eager to get their literary career started, spending some time doing something else after completing their education was not a bad idea. In fact, a good number of recent college graduates, many of them English majors, later realized that the terrible job they had to take fresh out of school turned out to be a godsend. When his Plan A (becoming a New York City policeman) did not materialize, for example, Michael Ledwidge took a job as a doorman at a Park Avenue building, finding it to be a degrading experience. But the job provided excellent fodder for an aspiring crime novelist like himself, he discovered, using conservations with the snobbish tenants as material to inform his work. An inordinate number of crime novels and thrillers cast some wealthy madman as the villain (think James Bond films), but Ledwidge thought an anonymous worker with a master plan to make a big score was much more compelling. Spending time with tenants in their fabulous apartments (he had access to their keys) sparked many felonious ideas that he subsequently used in his novels that were sold to major publishers. "Imagination, observation and extrapolation focused on the everyday can be the basis for stories that are stronger the less outlandish they seem, because they are comprised of elements readily recognizable," he explained, adding that, "sometimes, the worse the job, the more interesting it is."[14]

There were other benefits of having a supplemental, non-literary life for certain kinds of writers. Having some kind of job typically allowed some interaction with other people, lessening the isolation that came with writing. Being alone for long periods of time was the most common complaint among many writers, especially those who had previously worked in a group setting like an office. Some writers working at home found themselves talking to their cat or dog, missing even the tedious company holiday parties that they had once so disdained. Surrounding oneself with people when working was the logical solution for more social types. Laptop nomads found that writing at coffeehouses not only helped with the isolation blues but was a way to separate work from home, a healthy thing that provided more balance between one's personal and professional life. As well, there were more chat rooms on the Internet just for writers popping up (some even dedicated to specific genres like romance, science fiction, and mystery), these too a way to engage with other human beings. Other writers (and artists) were renting space in a collective office, finding that being home was not conducive to a good work ethic and that sitting in a coffeehouse all day was too distracting (or simply got them too caffeinated).[15]

Even writers stuck in a room by themselves could very well feel connected to other people through their work, however, sometimes more so than if they held a job in a group setting. Although their fictional characters existed only in memory or imagination, it was not unusual for novelists to report feeling deep and meaningful relationships with these "people," something that was overshadowed by the often-cited solitude of the job. A writer might experience a wide range of emotions involving a wide variety of individuals in a single session, making one wonder if the occupation was as lonely as usually acknowledged. "Writing makes you feel less alone and more alive," stated Rebecca Troyer Robbins of Bloomington, Indiana, winner of *Writer* magazine's 2003 Writer/Journey Conference essay contest whose topic was "Why I Write." Robbins had had other jobs surrounded by real people, but found that writing allowed her to "fit into a larger universe" as she worked by herself in the room over her garage. Like many writers, she felt compelled to observe and record the world around her and to make sense of it, an urge that was, in a word, "irresistible."[16]

Writers Rule

Happily, those with the irresistible urge to write had new opportunities to become authors. Self-publishing had always been around, of course, but a new kind of respectability became attached to the practice with the rise of the Internet. More self-publishing websites designed to help writers become authors were appearing online in the early 2000s, challenging the traditional model of how books were developed, marketed, and distributed. There were a number of reasons why self-publishing made sense for some writers. Self-publishing gave writers complete creative control, and was a much faster way to get a book into the marketplace. Many writers choosing to self-publish intended to use their book as a tool to promote a consulting or other kind of business, meaning they needed a lot of copies that would be costly to buy from a traditional publisher (even at the substantial author discount). As well, major publishers did not do a very good job marketing books for authors who were not on their "A-list," making many question the wisdom of signing away most of the potential royalties. Last, and perhaps most important, writers who self-published could potentially make much more money than by going the traditional route because they kept 100 percent of the royalties rather than the standard 10 percent or thereabouts.[17]

Another big reason to self-publish was, of course, the difficulty of selling a book to an existing publisher. As it always had been, the publishing business was not particularly welcome to new writers, with the usual barriers to entry making it unlikely that many books would ever see the light of day unless self-published. Landing a literary agent—something that was virtually required for an editor at a major publishing house to consider one's work—was itself quite challenging. Agents took on only those writers whose work they considered marketable and who already had a "platform," i.e., the credentials deemed necessary to make them legitimate authors. After rejection after rejection from agents and/or editors, many writers were understandably thrilled to have the opportunity to become authors by publishing their book themselves. Books were also known to get "orphaned" when their respective commissioning editor left or got fired from a traditional publisher, another reason to self-publish. How many books one sold was often incidental to the self-published author; just holding the thing (and seeing it listed on Amazon) could very well be satisfaction for all the time, effort, and money invested in the project. Handing out copies to friends and family was another joyful experience, with perhaps a talk at the local bookstore icing on the cake.

While some bloggers were self-publishing books, major publishers were actively courting others who had a big following or unique take on a particular subject. Blogging was a key way for writers to establish an online presence and build their all-important platform. A new genre had even emerged—the "blook," or book by a blogger. Publishers were increasingly interested in blogs (online journals usually written by an individual or small group in an informal, conversational style) because the material seemed fresher and more energetic than that of a typical nonfiction book. More popular blogs may also have been stealing potential book buyers, making some publishers conclude that if you can't beat 'em, join 'em. Liberal political commentator Markos Moulitsas of dailykos.com was getting about half a million hits in 2006, making it not surprising that he landed a major blook deal for his *Crashing the Gate*. As self-publishing became more respectable because of the Internet, so were books based on blogs. The first Lulu Blooker Prize was awarded that year to the best Web-connected book, a sign of bloggers' new status in traditional publishing.[18]

For Michael Kinsley, however, the best thing about any kind of Internet-based writing was that there were fewer editors. Kinsley, the

Chapter 5 • The Nomads, 2000–

American political journalist, had a major beef with magazine and newspaper editors, thinking that they over-revised the work of writers. It was true that editors often cut words from an article, essay, or review, sometimes brutally, a slicing and dicing that Kinsley believed violated the writer's intent and thus ruining the piece. (Kinsley had himself served as an editor for print-based media, but believed he was one of the good—meaning minimalist—ones.) Happily, editors were rare on blogs and online forums, allowing writers to be masters of their creative domain, just as it should be. "Writers rule, and a thought can go straight from your head onto the Net," he wrote in his column in *Time* in 2008, considering the dearth of editors in the online universe to be "heaven."[19]

In addition to the new urgency among writers to blog and create their own websites in order to promote themselves and their work, podcasts were becoming an increasingly popular way to leverage new media. Podcasts were and are sound files distributed over the Internet that users could listen to on personal computers or portable media players. Some authors were serializing one of their books via podcasts in order to build an audience for their next one, while others talked about their craft or hosted a radio show. Turning listeners into book buyers was the primary goal, with podcasting allowing thousands of people to get to know the author and his or her work. Like blogs, podcasts were a great way to attract a literary agent and land a deal; the ability to tell an agent or publisher one already had tens of thousands of followers was just the kind of thing each wanted to hear when considering a book proposal.[20] After getting over a hundred rejection letters for his novels over the course of fifteen years, for example, a writer named Scott Sigler decided to podcast them, over time creating a large enough following for a publisher to give him a three-book deal. "The podcast meant I wasn't just another author," Sigler explained his success; "I was a friend who wrote good books."[21]

Not just getting a book published but marketing it was radically transformed as the Internet evolved. In the new digital publishing landscape, writers were advised to take a "multiplatform" approach in the development and marketing of their "content." By planting portions of a book or other literary property in a variety of media, experts in the online universe pointed out, authors had a better chance of having "users" discover their material. The video website YouTube was a perfect opportunity to allow potential readers to sample one's work, with relevant blogs another way to get exposure with otherwise difficult to reach audiences. As a plus, developers of video games, films, and television shows were known to cruise the Internet in search for promising properties, more reason why American writers should go digital.[22]

Song of Myself

For certain authors, greater exposer due to the Internet meant something different than scoring multi-book deals or perhaps reaching the top 1,000 on Amazon's rankings. Some (male) writers freely admitted that they chose the profession at least in part because they believed it would attract women. Published authors were admittedly a long way from being rock stars in terms of fame (or, I would venture, sex appeal), but women were known to develop crushes on writers whose work they admired. Readers often felt they knew authors because a book could be so personally revealing (or interpreted that way), making the former want to meet the latter in person. Author photos also could make readers wish they could hook up with such a dreamboat (although, as on dating websites, the real thing usually turned out to be significantly less dreamy). Popular authors like David Foster Wallace even had "groupies" who went to readings in hopes some romantic connection could be made with the obviously funny, sensitive man. Jonathan Safran Foer was another author whose smarts and coolness were making women swoon (one critic labeled him "the precious young prince of wit-lit"),[23] suggesting that there may have been some validity to writers thinking their chosen occupation could serve as an aphrodisiac.[24]

While some writers' saw their books as the means to amorous ends, it's safe to say that the majority were interested in more commercial matters. Authors were known to become different people when a new book of theirs was published, as the desire to earn back their advance became somewhat of an obsession. Anyone and everyone in or with a possible connection to the media (especially Oprah, Terry

Chapter 5 • The Nomads, 2000–

Gross, or *The Today Show*) was considered fair game for authors or their publicists to contact. Authors who could afford it often hired an outside publicist to complement the marketing plan orchestrated by the publisher. Social media had become extremely important in spreading the news about a new book, making Facebook and Twitter the twenty-first century version of once influential print publications like the *Saturday Review of Literature*. A positive review was good news, of course, except for it producing a hunger for more. "It's a feedback loop, and it's totally addictive," as the nonfiction author Mary Roach described the voracious appetite for good reviews. Googling oneself a dozen or more times a day to see if any new reviews had been posted online was not unusual, with checking one's ranking on Amazon even more compulsive. Authors asking friends and relatives to post five-star reviews of their new book on the websites of online bookstores to encourage sales was judged not entirely unethical, nor was the moving of their baby to the front of a bookstore or making its shelf display more prominent.[25]

While virtually no effort to sell more books was considered out of bounds, contemporary American novelists were frequently taken to task for what critics viewed as a self-indulgent writing style. Tom Wolfe continued to complain that his colleagues were infusing their work with too much of their personal selves and not enough social reality, a legitimate claim perhaps given works like Wallace's brash *Infinite Jest* and Bret Easton Ellis's entire me-based oeuvre. (The protagonist in his 2005 *Lunar Park* was actually named Bret Easton Ellis.) But it could be argued that there was a long tradition of egotism within American literature, ranging from Walt Whitman's *Song of Myself* to Saul Bellow's *The Adventures of Augie March* to much of Philip Roth's work. Was it necessarily bad for writers to literally put themselves first in their novels? David Amsden didn't think so. "We seem to have forgotten that all books are (overtly or covertly) portraits of narcissists brought to us on a tidal wave of writerly megalomania," he suggested in *New York* in 2005, seeing authors as "rock stars playing on a stage in their minds."[26]

The problem with James Frey, however, was that he did not put enough of his real self in what was presented as a memoir. The controversy surrounding Frey's 2006 bestseller *A Million Little Pieces* was not contained to the publishing industry; the story became the subject of water cooler conversation for raising the question of whether memoirs had to be entirely (or in Frey's case, mostly) truthful. (Frey had promoted his confessional book on Oprah's television show, with the host later saying she and her millions of viewers had been "betrayed" by the author.) Was there any room for fiction in a memoir (literally, a collection of memories), or did all autobiography by definition have to be 100 percent factual? There was no doubt that Frey certainly stretched the truth in the book, the online investigation site The Smoking Gun disclosed, and eventually the author admitted he had made up many of the details of his life for dramatic effect. Soon after the scandal, there were accusations that Augusten Burroughs had made up parts of his memoir *Running with Scissors*, further adding to the conversation about the blurrier-than-believed lines between nonfiction and fiction.[27]

Truth enhancers' desperation to make a mark in the literary world could be seen as another example of how writing at its most fundamental level was, to paraphrase Whitman, a song of oneself. The notion that writing was at its heart an act of personal expression (or, if you prefer, egotism, narcissism, or megalomania) was also made evident by the putting out of as much work as humanly possible. Some American writers were legitimately assigned the label of "prolific," making one wonder if publishing a couple dozen or more books in as many years was rooted in a kind of compulsion. Joyce Carol Oates had written more than a hundred books in forty-five years, for example, and John Updike about sixty in fifty years. Popular novelists like Dean Koontz, Danielle Steel, and James Patterson also turned out books at an alarming rate, their prolificacy certainly helping them to build their brands and literary franchises. Romance novelist Barbara Cartland was the contemporary queen of productivity, however, having written some 700 books and, reportedly, having 160 more in the can at the time of her death. "Truly extreme productiveness (like its opposite) is beyond the absolute control of the author," posited Geoff Nicholson (no slouch at twenty books in twenty-two years), reasonably suggesting that some unknown force accounted for the inability to stop writing.[28]

As in any field, extreme productiveness in writing was directly correlated with a strong (perhaps too strong) work ethic. Prolific writers, especially those of fiction, were inclined to be able to produce many words at a sitting regardless of whether they had what athletes sometimes referred to as their A-game. Less fortunate (and more average) novelists relied heavily on those moments when scenes, characters, and dialog flowed like water from their brains to their writing instrument of choice. In those instances, writers had to quickly record the movie that was playing in their head, as they knew it would not last long and then in all likelihood be forever gone. Even if the muse arrived in the middle of the night, it was best to get the flash of brilliance down on paper or in Word, if only because it would be hard to get back to sleep after such a jolt of creativity. A good many writers kept flashlights, note pads, and pens by their beds just for those occasions, and scribbled away as if one was simply taking dictation. Making sense out of the stream of consciousness when daylight came was a whole other matter; what one thought was perfectly legible at 3:30 a.m. often turned out to resemble a Jackson Pollock painting just hours later.[29]

The converse of such fruitful literary yields in the wee hours was the dreaded arrival of what fantasy-adventure novelist Lisa Shearin called "the Anti-Muse." As the evil twin of the goddess of inspiration, the Anti-Muse made her appearance known in order to do everything in her power to convince the writer that his or her work-in-progress was, in a word, crap. One's entire literary career was a fraud, she asserted, and the truth of such would be revealed with the publication of this next book. Writers struggling with a particular work were most prone towards having their personal Anti-Muse make an early morning house call. Whole chapters had to be revised, and there were dozens of weak spots throughout the work, she whispered into the ears of now very awake writers, this too making additional sleep unlikely. Thankfully, the Anti-Muse was usually nowhere to be found by daylight, and the writer was no longer convinced that he or she should seek out alternative employment options as she had suggested.[30]

The Rubber-Chicken Circuit

Given how difficult it was to make a good living as a full-time author, even writers on good terms with their muse often wondered if they should have chosen another career path. Because they were literally money in the bank (versus royalties, which depended on sales), advances were understandably considered a very important part of any book deal. Until around the 1960s, elite authors rarely asked for an advance, leaving that humbling experience to writers who really needed the money. But with the cost of living going up and up and up, all writers became eager to get a check upfront to pay their expenses while they completed their book. Huge advances emerged in the 1970s, when publishers gobbled up the paperback rights for hardcover books that had done well. Advances shrank after the binge of the 1980s and when the industry went though relatively hard times on the 1990s. By 2009, publishers were still crying poor but occasionally awarded big advances, some in the millions of dollars, for the simple reason that they needed to sell good books or they would eventually go out of business. Seven out of ten titles did not earn back their advance, making publishers count on the three that did to put them in the black.[31]

Exact figures were rarely reported, but it was believed that the average advance offered for a trade title by a major publisher was around $30,000 in 2009. Given that an author could take years to write a book (and that an advance was usually doled out in three chunks), $30,000 was hardly a lot of money for most people to live on. (In 2010, the poverty income guideline for family of four was about $23,000, according to the U.S. Census Bureau, making the average book advance not much more than that.) Even a six-figure advance was not really much of a windfall if one considered the other side of the balance sheet. Dave Eggers revealed that he received a $100,000 advance for his *A Heartbreaking Work of Staggering Genius* but, after his all expenses (including a 15 percent agent commission and self-employment tax), was left with just a $40,000 profit. Add nice things like health insurance (and a desk to write on), and it became clear that even for a top author, writing remained a middle class job in financial terms.[32]

As always, authors looked for ways to make money beyond advances and royalties for books they had written. Speaking to groups was a natural fit for authors with expertise in a particular area, and an excellent source of supplementary income. "In recent years, a growing number of writers, from the best-selling to the less so, have hit the

Chapter 5 • The Nomads, 2000–

rubber-chicken circuit," the *New York Times* reported in 2008; the fact that authors were often not very good speakers (brain scans showed they were actually "smarter" when sticking to their profession) did not seem to diminish their demand.[33] B-list authors could pick up a couple of grand for an hour or so talk, while A-listers like presidential historian Doris Kearns Goodwin made as much as $40,000 for the same. (Businesspeople could learn a lot from Lincoln, she contended.) In speaking to groups for a fee, contemporary authors were carrying on a long literary tradition; Mark Twain had orated in large venues across the country to make some much-needed cash, and Ralph Waldo Emerson received payment for lecturing in Boston. Seeing the demand, some major publishers had formed their own speaker bureaus, the side benefit being that their authors would likely sell more books at events. Authors were divided when it came to talking in front of a group. Some authors were happy (or at least willing) to give talks at rich people's birthday parties if there was money to be made, while others considered any encounter with the general public to be a painful and thus avoided-at-all-costs experience.[34]

With so much money being made by those fortunate enough to work in a profession that paid well (hedge funds had replaced dot-coms as the best opportunity to get rich), writers remained fully aware that their job was an interesting but financially dubious one. Even children of writers somehow knew that their father's or mother's profession was not a particularly good way to earn a living. Author Paul Greenberg recounted this funny yet irritating joke his teenage daughter told him:

<small>WOMAN: What do you do?
MAN: Me? Oh, I write books.
WOMAN: How interesting! Have you sold anything recently?
MAN: Why, yes. My couch, my car and my flat-screen television.[35]</small>

With such jokes going around, writers were considered losers in American society, Greenberg reasonably concluded, an unfair assessment given that money was not the only way to measure the worth of an occupation or individual. What was the solution to this problem? A national bailout, he half-joked, thinking something along the lines of FDR's Federal Writer's Project would go a long way towards helping writers recover some of the respect and financial stability they deserved. (That 1930s project paid some 6,000 unemployed writers to write various materials with the underlying mission to "describe America to Americans.") Part of the problem was that there continued to be simply too many writers or people that wanted to be one. There were currently about 185,000 Americans who supported themselves primarily by writing, a 2008 National Endowment for the Arts survey revealed, an oversupply in purely economic terms. With so many writers out there willing to take whatever money was available, in other words, there was little incentive for publishers to pay large sums for any particular book or article except a possible bestseller. Too much product was another problem. Roughly 275,000 new titles and editions were being published in the United States each year, according to the industry source Bowker, a figure also suggesting that writer capacity exceeded reader demand.[36]

Joe Queenan could personally vouch that too many Americans wanted to be authors even if they would serve as the butt of jokes in such a money-minded age. The humorous cultural critic was constantly handed manuscripts to read, even by his hairdresser. Rather than simply say no, something most well known authors had always done in these cases, Queenan often agreed, a decision he always later regretted. Ritual dismemberment of a body was a more-common-than-one-might-have-thought literary theme among amateur writers, he informed readers of *The Weekly Standard* in 2010, as were supernatural retellings of *Romeo and Juliet* and ancient classics reimagined with mafia characters. Queenan also received numerous query letters from writers that he immediately forwarded to a literary agent who was a personal friend. Somehow, these ideas for books were more awful than the manuscripts he was handed, with an unusual number featuring vampires, mermaids, and, worst of all, writers' dogs. Random House had recently made it known that it had not accepted an unsolicited, un-agented manuscript from the slush pile in two decades, more evidence that there was, as always, an oversupply of writers in the United States.[37] Still, many more American writers were on the way. There were 854 university programs in creative writing offering a master of fine arts (MFA) degree in 2010—more than ten times the 79 to be found in the United States in 1975.[38]

Even accomplished authors sometimes wondered whether they

Chapter 5 • The Nomads, 2000–

should be in the business. Many authors felt a sense of euphoria when completing a book, but that certainly wasn't the case for Joseph Epstein, a nonfiction author. Rather, Epstein's strongest feeling after writing the final word was "doubt," specifically whether he had done justice to the book's subject. There was no definitive answer to the question, making the process of writing for him ultimately a not entirely fulfilling experience. Soon after starting a book, in fact, Epstein began to wonder if his intellectual grasp of the subject was as robust as he had originally thought. Midway through a project, he ruminated if he should have embarked on the journey in the first place, thinking perhaps he should just call it quits. (Esteemed American writers including John Updike, Saul Bellow, Truman Capote, Harper Lee, Michael Chabon, Junot Diaz, Jennifer Egan, and Stephen King had each aborted works well in progress or threw entire first drafts away.[39]) The fact that he would have to return the advance money to the publisher should he ditch the project was incentive enough for Epstein to keep going, however, as was his determination to not admit defeat.[40]

One might expect having completed a first draft would have made Epstein happy, but not so. Instead, Epstein, who wrote essays and short stories as well often under the pen name Aristides, was rather appalled at what he had produced, now convinced that his once promising venture had been mostly a failure. The work was filled with repetitions, for one thing, and, perhaps worse, profoundly stylistically challenged. It was easy for him to spot which particular mornings he was on and which he was off, not a good thing in terms of continuity or flow. But there was a saving grace for Epstein: revision. Like many authors, Epstein enjoyed the revision process, more so in fact than the writing of the first draft. Revision offered the chance to fix all the many flaws in a book, whether they be absurdly long run-on sentences, wrong spellings, and grammar that did not adhere to what was generally accepted as English. Even such repairs did not make Epstein content with what he had first set out to do, however. Now that he had written a book on a particular subject, he was prepared to write a much better one on that same subject, a highly impractical proposition on many levels. By that point, anyway, Epstein had an exciting idea for a new book, and promptly began the whole, troublesome voyage all over again.[41]

Who Needs a Publisher?

Fortunately, the relentless drive to write a book, whether grounded in getting some attention, making a little money, or simply to offer one's take on a certain subject, can now be easily satisfied regardless of the outcome. Self-publishing has exploded in recent years, good news to the millions of American writers for whom finding an agent or publisher for their project did not work out. Uploading one's book to Amazon's online Kindle store reached a kind of tipping point around 2010, allowing writers bypassing the traditional model of publishing to let the world know they had become authors. Even better, self-publishing had gained considerably greater respect from reviewers and booksellers, with much of the indignity of choosing a "vanity press" to publish one's work dissipated. Even some bestsellers were popping up in the Kindle store, which by then was actually outselling Amazon's hardcover sales. More print-on-demand services like Lulu and CreateSpace were appearing online, further challenging the strictly volume-based business platform of major publishers. "Who needs a publisher?" asked *Newsweek* that year, as more authors opted to self-publish much in part for the 70 to 80 percent of revenue to be realized versus the 8 to 9 percent standard royalty rate. A low price and favorable user-generated ratings were the keys to an e-book's success, according to such literary nomads, some of them earning (or claiming to earn) six-figure incomes from their writing.[42]

The expansion of the online universe over the past decade has gone much further than the spike in self-publishing. "The Internet has exposed writers to a level of personal scrutiny formerly reserved for pop stars and teen idols," reported *Newsweek* in 2010, with blogs and websites such as gossipy Gawker informing readers once-secret information like advance figures and even how well-known authors spent their windfalls. (Jonathan Safran Foer used his from his second novel, *Extremely Loud and Incredibly Close*, to purchase a $6 million Brooklyn brownstone, it was revealed, much to readers' scorn. Writers, or at least good ones, they apparently figured, should not enjoy luxurious accommodations.) Wunderkind Jonathan Franzen was also taking a beating online, now considered overly pretentious and peevish as reader familiarity with the author of *The Corrections* and his recently

Chapter 5 • The Nomads, 2000–

published *Freedom* bred contempt. Franzen occasionally wrote in a sensory-deprivation chamber while also earmuffed and blindfolded, it became known, just the kind of information trollers of the Internet pounced on.[43]

The rise of the Internet had another unfortunate consequence for many writers: even lower pay, at least according to some observers of the scene. The mad rush for content, i.e., copy for websites, had not bettered the already feeble economic lot for writers but, paradoxically, apparently made it worse. While the literary universe did indeed become more democratic and autonomous as it shifted online, it also lowered the pay for freelance writing to be posted on websites. "Writers are the only people I know who are expected to work for next to nothing or nothing," observed Leon Wieseltier in *The New Republic* in 2010, a strange situation given that much of the Internet would not exist without writers. Writers were arguably more in demand than ever because of the insatiable appetite of the Internet, Wieseltier argued, but their financial compensation had hit rock bottom. The plethora of free online content had also helped to lower advances for books published by major houses, adding to writers' money woes. ("$30,000 is the new $100,000," one New York literary agent had recently remarked in reference to the average advance.) The much mocked digs of the proverbial uncompromising artist—the unheated garret in a walkup tenement—was now itself unaffordable, Wieseltier noted, thinking the digital revolution had done no favors for writers, at least in financial terms.[44]

Some freelancers, however, were clearly benefiting monetarily from the new writing opportunities to be found online. A good number of corporations, publishers, and well-funded start-ups had decent-sized budgets for bloggers, making work-for-hire blogging the twenty-first century version of the lucrative magazine article writing of the past. Rates varied immensely, but some bloggers were regularly making $5,000 a month for creating much needed content, not bad at all given the pay scale of freelance writing. Some companies were trying to save money by using electronic bloggers (that recycled posts from other websites), but found that only a human was capable of providing quality content that attracted users. Rather than being a generalist, having a niche or singular focus was the ideal way to make money from blogging, experts pointed out, with the tried and true formula of being able to turn a piece around quickly another key asset.[45]

Creating content for other "alternative" literary outlets was another good way to be a professional writer if one was determined to be one. It may have lacked the "glamour" and prestige of being an author, blogger, or even magazine article freelancer, but writing copy for brochures and other marketing communications paid real money. A wide variety of organizations—small businesses, retailers, hospitals, universities, and nonprofits—typically published such materials as well as press releases and newsletters, keeping a good number of writers very busy. Annual reports and speechwriting were other opportunities to produce words and, at the same time, avoid the wild, often disappointing world of book publishing. "Displaced" journalists were increasingly drawn to such opportunities after being downsized from a newspaper or magazine, with writing advertising copy on a freelance basis a complementary sideline. The skill set required writing for alternative outlets—researching, developing stories, interviewing, and working under deadlines—was essentially the same as for traditional publishing, i.e., books and magazines, making one who chose the former path every bit a professional writer as a bestselling novelist.[46]

Wax and Wane

The scrappiness required to be a laptop nomad today has encouraged a vigorous how-to discourse within the writing community that is heavily informed by therapeutic and self-help thinking and language. Through books, magazine articles, and blogs, writers are advised (by other writers, of course) to follow any number of steps to be a better, more successful practitioner of the craft. Recent topics or lessons include: the setting of goals, being a jack-of-all-trades, discovering one's own writer's retreat, avoiding author burnout, using one's social intelligence, staying positive, establishing oneself as an expert, doing nothing for a few minutes each day, coping with rejection, shaking things up when one was stuck, finding inspiration, creating one's own rules, combating negativity and self-doubt, and, last but not least, how to

Chapter 5 • The Nomads, 2000–

handle people who tell one not to be a writer. Writers are indeed a sensitive bunch, one would reasonably conclude after taking a gander at their trade literature, seemingly in need of constant need of motivational support and feel-good advice.

Perhaps due to the nation's aging population, considerable attention has also recently been given to older American writers and, specifically, whether they were still capable of producing good work. Authors many times experienced diminishing returns after some initial success, it had been acknowledged for decades, raising the question of why it was so difficult for even the best of writers to sustain a long literary career. Novelists often got out of the starting blocks quickly with their first published works but, once established, seemed to lose their way and bring forth less interesting stories. "After that first success," noted Susan Cheever, "most writers' imaginations seem to wax and wane at will despite the author's best efforts." One- or two-book wonders like Harper Lee or Joseph Heller were the most extreme examples of this racehorse-like fast-start, slow-finish phenomenon. Some novelists, fully aware of this, would write different kinds of books in order to keep fresh. Others, notably Norman Mailer, would switch genres late in their careers in order to get a second wind. (Louisa May Alcott had done the same, moving from fiction to memoir and then back to fiction to write *Little Women*.) Authors confessing their best writing years were behind them but kept going wondered if they should have stopped years ago despite the fact that they were qualified to do little else.[47]

Although perhaps filled with some self-doubt after enjoying considerable success, many older authors approached their writing process no differently despite their advanced age. At age 77, for example, Philip Roth made it clear that he was as passionate about his job as ever. In fact, older authors were more likely to stick to their guns when editors wanted to make changes to their material, having more experience knowing what would be best for the book. It was also not unusual for a publisher's marketing people to want a different (i.e., more catchy) title, something a young author was inclined to readily agree to out of respect for a professional's expertise and knowing business was not his or her forte. Writers of a certain age often regretted such a decision, however, convinced that their original title was truer to the story, and fiercely battled such suggestions when they arose later in their careers. While one's energy level and ability to retrieve words could each be less than they once had been, one's literary instincts were almost always better, not too bad a tradeoff.[48]

Writers who had begun their literary careers well before the arrival of the Internet were of course keenly aware how much the business had changed in recent decades. In an age of real-time blogging, video gaming, and relentless e-mailing and texting, it was easy to proclaim the death of the two-hundred-page-plus book, or at least the Great American Novel. Readers just no longer had the patience or time to digest such a tome, it was often argued. But such a proclamation was hardly new; the eclipse of the modernists nearly a century ago brought forth widespread lamenting that fiction as we knew it had expired. History suggested that the novel was more difficult to kill than Rasputin. The literary output of American novelists including Michael Chabon and Junot Diaz in the fall of 2012 alone was proof enough that the book was, at least for the moment, still alive and well. Writing for *Esquire* that year, Stephen Marche made the case that despite all the whining about the state of publishing, prospects for the American writer were rarely better. The Internet may have effectively destroyed many industries, notably the music business, he pointed out, but a fair number of writers were prospering despite (or perhaps due to) technological change. Tom Wolfe had recently received a $7 million advance for his latest novel, one sign that publishers were not about to all go belly up. In fact, revenues for both hardcovers and paperbacks were up, as e-readers created a new market rather than wiped out the existing one, something many had predicted.[49]

Going well against the grain, Marche was positively gung-ho on the state of publishing in America, both traditional and alternative. Writers just starting out had opportunities those of previous generations could only dream about, Marche opined, having unprecedented access to the marketplace. The e-book *Fifty Shades of Grey*, for example, was not just a literary blockbuster that further de-stigmatized self-publishing but a cultural phenomenon, and something that was likely not possible a generation ago. Small presses were publishing wonderful books that were more available than ever, he added, something backed up by McPherson & Company's winning of the National Book Award in 2010 and Bellevue Literary Press's being awarded the Pulitzer Prize for Fiction that same year. Not just book publishers but magazine publishers were in a healthy place, according to Marche. Essays or long-form nonfiction that regularly appeared in *The New Yorker*, *Esquire*, and other highbrow magazines were just as or even better written than in the all-too-fondly-remembered good old days. Journalism too was enjoying a heyday, with the reporting found on certain websites and innumerable blogs top-notch. "A massive process of literary rebirth is under way," Marche pronounced, taking issue with all the Chicken Littles claiming that writing had become an all-but-dead art form in the early twenty-first century.[50]

Those filing tax returns for the world's highest paid authors would confirm Marche's thesis that it was very good times for writers, at least extremely popular ones. The top three authors, based on annual income, were all Americans; James Patterson made $89 million between June 2014 and June 2015, according to *Forbes*, while number 2 John Green and number 3 Veronica Roth earned $26 million and $25 million respectively over that same period. Patterson's income was in part a function of his amazing output, having no less than eighteen books earning advances or royalties. Green and Roth, meanwhile, made their own fortunes without publishing a single word during that time frame, with each Young Adult (YA) author selling millions of copies from their backlist. As well, movies were made based on adaptations of the latter two authors' novels, providing an additional source of revenue and driving additional book sales.[51] In hot pursuit for the next Patterson, Green, or Roth, major publishers were now frequently offering seven-figure advances, more evidence that it was halcyon days for those writers able to produce highly commercial material.[52]

Cultivating Thought

Seeing such numbers, thousands, perhaps millions of American writers have continued to pursue their dream of being part of the literary elite, another thing that has not changed since the days of Fitzgerald and Hemingway. Unpublished writers convinced they had produced the Great American Novel but were having trouble making publishers believe that no doubt looked to Garth Risk Hallberg as inspiration. A number of publishers engaged in a bidding war for Hallberg's debut, 900+ page novel, *City on Fire*, which ultimately sold for $2 million to Knopf. Hallberg, a 36-year-old who grew up in Greenville, North Carolina, was following in the footsteps of some other American writers who had spent years in obscurity before hitting it big, such as John Irving, Don DeLillo, and Jonathan Franzen. New York City played an important role in fueling Hallberg's imagination. "I always thought, 'When I grow up, I'm going to move to the big city and become a writer,' because that's what writers did," Hallberg said after creating what some in the media were calling "the literary event of the year." Hallberg, now following form by living in a heavily hipster-populated section of Brooklyn, was inspired as a child by *Harriet the Spy* and *Stuart Little*, books that were, like his own, set in Manhattan. *City of Fire* was being likened to Tom Wolfe's *Bonfire of the Vanities*, more confirmation that the Great American Novel (and the kind of social novel that Wolfe hoped other American authors would write) was still being published. Like the debut novels of many past authors who received large advances, Hallberg's (who the *New York Times* called "The Literary Wunderkind of the Year") received mixed reviews and sold only moderately well. By January 2016, *City on Fire* had sold about 80,000 copies, far short of the estimated 300,000 copies needed to break even.[53]

The seven-figure advance Max Brallier received that same year for his series of books with the unlikely title *Galactic Hot Dogs* was another good example of how American writers could still become rich and famous, particularly if they fully leveraged the new model of publishing. The children's book published by Aladdin, an imprint of Simon & Schuster, was based on a story originally found on Funbrain.com, a popular gaming site that served as an incubator for traditional publishing. It was clear that Aladdin was trying to repeat history. A decade earlier, Jeff Kinney's *Diary of a Wimpy Kid* series had been similarly offered for free on Funbrain, ultimately selling more than 150 million copies when published in print. More than six million kids had already read the online version of *Galactic Hot Dogs* (about a boy who, along with his team of a robot, a headstrong princess, and a clumsy alien, fight giant mutant worms and zombie space pirates), just the kind of

Chapter 5 • The Nomads, 2000–

pre-existing fan base publishers like to see before investing big bucks into a book. "We've seen this model work before," said Mara Anastas, vice president and publisher of Aladdin, "the groundwork is already laid."[54] Three books in the *Galactic Hot Dog* series have to-date been published (*Cosmoe's Weiner Getaway, The Weiner Strikes Back,* and *Revenge of the Space Pirates*), an indication that Simon & Schuster has every intention of earning back its big advance.

Such success stories demonstrate that while it may or may not be a golden age for the American writer as Stephen Marche contested, great things are indeed possible. While the chances of becoming wealthy by being an author today remain slim at best (see Neal Gabler's fascinating May 2016 essay in *The Atlantic*, "The Secret Shame of Middle-Class Americans," to see how even successful, well-known writers like he is cash-poor),[55] one can still find thriving literary communities and places in which the written word is celebrated. The Lillian Vernon Creative Writers House in Greenwich Village is such a place; any given night one might hear Jonathan Lethem, Junot Diaz, or some of the country's best poets read from one of their works, and the old building houses NYU's Creative Writing Program (in which Joyce Carol Oates is among the faculty and Garth Risk Hallberg is among the recent graduates). Jonathan Safran Foer often writes (and naps) there, making it a throwback of sorts to the kind of bohemian club that Greenwich Village was once famous for.[56]

A new museum is serving as another literary beehive and a place that individuals can go to learn more about American writers and their work. The American Writers Museum opened its doors in Chicago in 2017, a much-deserved and long overdue happening given the important role that authors and their books have played in the nation's history. There are already a number of smaller museums devoted to certain literary genres or specific writers, but this institution is the first one dedicated to American authors' "influence on our history, our identity, our culture and our daily lives." The museum includes a "Visitors' Favorites" area where visitors are able to post their favorite books, authors, and quotes, as well as an interactive exhibit called "American Identity" featuring a chronology of the history of American literature. Displays dedicated to the most famous Americans authors such a Ralph Waldo Emerson, Harriet Beecher Stowe, and Walt Whitman are other

The American Writer

parts of the museum aimed at the more literary minded, as are sections focused on children's literature, westerns, mysteries, and other genres.[57]

Such a museum is very welcome given the passion many citizens of this country have for books, especially those written by other Americans, past and present. In his recent memoir *Avid Reader*, Robert Gottlieb described his lifelong love of reading and writing, having edited the works of such authors as Joseph Heller, Edna O'Brien, Nora Ephron, and Katherine Graham. Few, if any, people alive today have had such an intimate relationship with American literature, of course, but his experience illustrates the power of the written word in readers' lives.[58] The Library of Congress is perhaps the loudest cheerleader for American writers, doing yeoman's duty by recognizing the contribution that authors have made to the nation and to the lives of individuals over the years. In 2012, the Library launched an exhibition called "Books That Shaped America," with curators selecting 88 books that had a deep effect on life in this country. While that exhibition was running, visitors were given the opportunity to name other books by American authors that they found personally meaningful. Another exhibition called "America Reads" that featured 65 such books opened in 2016. While of course subjective, that list, in addition to the curated one, helped to get people talking about American writers and their work, precisely what is needed to keep literary culture relevant and vital.[59]

Celebrations of the American writer can also sometimes be found in unusual places. In 2015, Chipotle, the popular chain of Mexican restaurants, launched the second installment of its "Cultivating Thought" author series on its cups and bags. Like the first installment that ran the previous year, this one featured ten essays composed by notable writers, allowing diners to read mini-stories while they munched on burritos, tacos, and salads. (Check them out at cultivatingthought.com.) Jonathan Safran Foer returned as curator of the series, choosing works penned by Augusten Burroughs, Walter Isaacson, Amy Tan, Barbara Kingsolver, and others that took about two minutes to read. "We have always tried to use our packaging to engage with our customers' wit and intellect," remarked Mark Crumpacker, Chipotle's chief marketing and development officer, the campaign

Chapter 5 • The Nomads, 2000–

having the side benefit of exposing authors to consumers who might then be interested in reading one of their books. As well, the next great American writer may be inspired by something he or she read on a burrito bag, something even the clever folks at Chipotle may not have considered. Truth is, after all, stranger than fiction, leaving no doubt that the future of the American writer will be an interesting one.[60]

Chapter Notes

Introduction

1. Brand Whitlock, "Belgian and American Authors," *The Living Age*, January 6, 1923, 23.
2. Ben Tarnoff, *The Bohemians: Mark Twain and the San Francisco Writers Who Reinvented American Literature* (New York: Penguin, 2014).
3. Harold Bloom, *The Daemon Knows: Literary Greatness and the American Sublime* (New York: Spiegel & Grau, 2015).
4. Edward Mendeson, *Moral Agents: Eight Twentieth-Century American Writers* (New York: New York Review Books, 2015).
5. Richard Gray, *A History of American Literature* (Hoboken, NJ: Blackwell, 2004); Nina Baym (ed.), *The Norton Anthology of American Literature* (New York: W.W. Norton & Company, 2007); Greil Marcus and Werner Sollors, eds., *A New Literary History of America* (Cambridge, MA: Belknap Press, 2009).
6. Alfred Kazin, *God and the American Writer* (New York: Knopf, 1997); George Kimball and John Schulian, eds., *At the Fights: American Writers on Boxing* (New York: Library of America, 2012).
7. Thomas L. Masson, "Putting Our Literature on a Literary Basis," *The Bookman*, August 1919, 693.
8. Walter A. Dyer, "Distinguishing Insignia for Distinguished Authors," *The Bookman*, February 1919, 673.
9. Sacvan Bercovitch, *The American Jeremiad* (Madison: University of Wisconsin Press, 1978).
10. Chuck Leddy, "Writers Behaving Badly," *Writer*, March 2006, 8–9.
11. See Donald W. Goodwin, M.D., *Alcohol and the Writer* (New York: Penguin, 1990).
12. Olivia Laing, *The Trip to Echo Spring: On Writers and Drinking* (New York: Picador, 2014).
13. "Under the Influence," *Laphams Quarterly*, Spring 2010, 213.
14. Henry Hazlitt, "Our Greatest Authors," *Forum and Century*, October 1932, 245.
15. "The Point of View," *The Bookman*, March 1927, 1.

Chapter 1

1. Sherlock Bronson Gass, "Modernism and the Novel," *Forum*, May 1928, 757.
2. Brand Whitlock, "Belgian and American Authors," *The Living Age*, January 6, 1923, 23.
3. T.H.S. Escott, "American Literature Abroad," *The Living Age*, April 10, 1920, 94.
4. Louis Wann, "The Revolt From the Village in American Fiction," *Overland Monthly and Out West Magazine*, August 1925, 298.
5. Marshall Archibald, "A Browse Among the Best Sellers," *The Bookman*, September 1921, 8.

Chapter Notes—1

6. Bartlett Cormack, "Hail, Columbia!," *The Bookman*, January 1927, 568.
7. "Contemporary American Fiction," *The Bookman*, January 1923, 647.
8. Joseph Hergesheimer "The Feminine Nuisance in American Literature," *The Yale Review*, July 1921, 716, Frances Noyes Hart, "The Feminine Nuisance Replies," *The Bookman*, September 1921, 31.
9. Gertude Atherton, "The Alpine School of Fiction," *The Bookman*, March 1922, 26.
10. John Erskine, "Spotlight or Fame?," *The Bookman*, July 1922, 449.
11. "In Demand," *The Bookman*, May 1928, 249.
12. James Montgomery Flagg, "Pity the Successful Author!," *The Bookman*, December 1924, 469.
13. Joseph Lewis French, "Looking Backward," *The Bookman*, June 1926, 445.
14. Llewellyn Jones, "Chicago—Our Literary Crater," *The Bookman*, January 1925, 565.
15. "Chicago as the Literary Capital of the United States," *Current Opinion*, August 1920, 242.
16. Kenneth Burke, "Chicago and Our National Gesture," *The Bookman*, July 1923, 497.
17. Mrs. Frederick H. Colburn, "What Ails Bay Region Writers?," *Overland Monthly*, September 1927, 268.
18. Weare Holbrook, "The Corn Belt Renaissance," *Forum*, July 1924, 118.
19. DuBose Heyward, "The New Note in Southern Literature," *The Bookman*, April 1925, 153.
20. Hershel Brickell, "The Literary Awakening in the South," *The Bookman*, October 1927, 138.
21. Thomas L. Masson, "Has America a Literature?," *Forum*, March 1921, 348.
22. Paul Elmer More, "The Modern Current in American Literature," *Forum*, January 1928, 127.
23. "The Modern Current in American Literature."
24. Edna Ferber, "The Sketch Book," *The Bookman*, December 1926, 443.
25. "Modernism and the Novel."
26. Robert Herrick, "The Drift of the Current," *The Bookman*, December 1928, 377.
27. F. Scott Fitzgerald, "How to Waste Material," *The Bookman*, May 1926, 262.
28. Regis Michaud, "Insurgent American Literature," *The Living Age*, July 31, 1926, 251.
29. Charles W. Ferguson, "Five Rising Stars in American Fiction," *The Bookman*, May 1927, 251.
30. "Insurgent American Literature."
31. Mary Austin, "Sex in American Literature," *The Bookman*, June 1923, 385.
32. Guy Holt, "The Care and Feeding of Authors," *The Bookman*, December 1929, 349.
33. "The Care and Feeding of Authors."
34. "Authors are Awful," *The Bookman*, July 1931, 473.
35. Maristan Chapman, "The Trouble With Authors," *The Bookman*, December 1931, 368.
36. "The Truly Forgotten Man," *Forum and Century*, July 1935, 21.
37. J.B. Priestley, "Are Authors Human Beings?," *The Bookman*, April 1931, 137.
38. Arthur Train, "What Every Author Knows," *Saturday Evening Post*, January 24, 1931, 14.
39. Clarice Lorenz Aiken, "Literary Parasites," *The Bookman*, June 1930, 282.
40. "What Every Author Knows."
41. Osbert Burdett, "Is It Rash to Marry an Author?," *The Bookman*, April 1932, 49.
42. Eudora Ramsay Richardson, "Those Queer People Who Write," *The Bookman*, September 1931, 61.
43. I.A.R. Wylie, "As One Writer to Another," *Harper's Monthly*, February 1937, 268.
44. Sherwood Anderson, "So You Want to be a Writer?," *Saturday Review of Literature*, December 9, 1939, 13.

Chapter Notes—2

There was no confusion about Anderson's identity when he and four other notable American writers showed up unannounced at the White House on August 10, 1932 in hopes of meeting with President Herbert Hoover. The writers were there to protest the use of federal troops in evicting the "Bonus Army"—the thousands of World War I veterans and their families who had gathered in Washington that summer to demand cash payments for service certificates that could not be redeemed until 1945. The President refused to meet with the five writers, saying he was too busy. Hoover did have time to meet with a troop of Boy Scouts and a group of children wishing him birthday greetings (the President turned fifty-eight that day), however, making some wonder if his snubbing of the writers was politically motivated. Hoover accused the group of being Communists, a not uncommon accusation directed at leftish writers in the 1920s and 1930s. "Chronicle and Comment," *The Bookman*, October 1932, 564.

45. "So You Want to be a Writer?"
46. Dale Warren, "On the Working Habits of Authors," *The Bookman*, February 1930, 589.
47. George Jean Nathan, "The Best Place to Work," *Forum and Century*, July 1936, 39.
48. Osbert Burdett, "Is It Wise to Meet Authors?," *The Bookman*, August 1931, 586.
49. Clarence Budington Kelland, "Horse-Radish!," *Saturday Evening Post*, February 11, 1933, 21.
50. Louis Kronenberger, "Publisher's Reader," *The Bookman*, January 1933, 65.
51. "Publisher's Reader."
52. E. Arnot Robertson, "One Frightened Novelist," *Saturday Review of Literature*, July 20, 1935, 3.
53. Desmond MacCarthy, "The Bubble Reputation," *The Living Age*, October 1931, 162.
54. "Disappearing Novelists," *Saturday Review of Literature*, June 22, 1935, 8.
55. "Unemployed Writers," *Saturday Review of Literature*, October 31, 1936, 8.
56. Henry Hazlitt, "Our Greatest Authors," *Forum and Century*, October 1932, 245.
57. Homer Croy, "Selling Stories to the Movies," *Harper's Monthly*, December 1937, 96.
58. "The Pulitzer Prize in Fiction," *Saturday Review of Literature*, May 7, 1938, 8.
59. Arthur Train, "Rewards and Fairy Stories," *Saturday Review of Literature*, November 5, 1938, 3.
60. "Rewards and Fairy Stories."

Chapter 2

1. St. Clair McKelway, "Business Men, Get a Writer!," *Harper's Magazine*, August 1940, 270.
2. "Business Men, Get a Writer!"
3. "Open Letter to the Reading Public," *Saturday Review of Literature*, January 20, 1940, 4.
4. George Arliss, "Where Authors Become Writers," *Saturday Review of Literature*, March 30, 1940 14.
5. "Authors into Actors," *Saturday Review of Literature*, April 5, 1941, 15.
6. "Business Men, Get a Writer!"
7. J.W., "America Harbors 130,000,000 Writers," *Living Age*, December 1940, 358.
8. "America Harbors 130,000,000 Writers."
9. Pearl S. Buck, "Recognition and the Writer," *Saturday Review of Literature*, May 25, 1940, 13.
10. Charles Poore, "Checkbook Chekhovs," *New York Times Magazine*, October 5, 1941, SM13.
11. "Checkbook Chekhovs."
12. Elmer Davis, "The Economics of Authorship," *Saturday Review of Literature*, November 23, 1940, 4.

Chapter Notes—2

13. Norman Cousins, "Books are Not Enough," *Saturday Review of Literature*, September 21, 1940, 8.
14. M. Gumpert, "Hitler's Gift to America," *American Mercury*, July 1943, 49.
15. "Manifestos of Democracy," *Saturday Review of Literature*, August 2, 1941.
16. W. Roe, "Writers Go to War," *Writer*, March 1942, 86.
17. M. Christie, "Words are Weapons," *Independent Woman*, September 1943, 270.
18. John Erskine, "Women Don't Believe in Books," *Saturday Evening Post*, August 8, 1942, 28.
19. "Women Don't Believe in Books."
20. Osbert Sitwell, "What It Feels Like to Be an Author," *Saturday Review of Literature*, February 19, 1944, 6.
21. Louise Dickinson Rich, "What to Do When They Write," *Saturday Review of Literature*, January 8, 1944, 6.
22. John R. Tunis, "The Customer Always Writes," *Saturday Review of Literature*, October 6, 1945, 23.
23. "What to Do When They Write."
24. Harrison Smith, "A New World for Writers," *Saturday Review of Literature*, June 2, 1945, 16.
25. "A New World for Writers."
26. Paul Tabori, "Writer Meets People," *Saturday Review of Literature*, September 28, 1946, 36.
27. Ross Campbell, "Books and Ballyhoo," *Saturday Review of Literature*, May 24, 1947, 19.
28. "What's Wrong?," *Time*, August 4, 1947, 82.
29. John W. Aldridge, "America's Young Novelists," *Saturday Review of Literature*, February 12, 1949, 6.
30. Harrison Smith, "'Damn the Torpedoes!," *Saturday Review of Literature*, April 21, 1951, 22.
31. "America's Young Novelists."
32. R.B., "From Babbitt to the Bomb," *Saturday Review of Literature*, August 6, 1949, 100.
33. "'Damn the Torpedoes!"
34. C. Hartley Grattan, "The Trouble with Books Today," *Harper's Magazine*, November 1951, 33.
35. R.C. Hutchinson, "If One Must Write Fiction," *Saturday Review of Literature*, September 3, 1949, 6.
36. "Belles-Lettres," *Saturday Review of Literature*, June 30, 1951, 11.
37. "If One Must Write Fiction."
38. "The Trouble with Books Today."
39. J.K. Lasser, "Writer's Cramp on the Long Form," *Saturday Review of Literature*, March 11, 1950, 21.
40. Bennett Cerf, "Trade Winds," *Saturday Review of Literature*, March 3, 1951, 4.
41. Malcolm Cowley, "Psychoanalysts and Writers," *Harper's Magazine*, September 1954, 87.
42. Bernard DeVoto, "The Sixty-Cent Royalty," *Harper's Magazine*, January 1952, 41.
43. Elmer Rice, "The Industrialization of the Writer," *Saturday Review of Literature*, April 12, 1952, 13.
44. Tennessee Williams, "A Writer's Quest for a Parnassus," *New York Times Magazine*, August 13, 1950, SM9.
45. Harold Strauss, "The Illiterate American Writer," *Saturday Review of Literature*, May 17, 1952, 8.
46. Louis Auchincloss, "On Meeting Authors," *Saturday Review of Literature*, June 19, 1954, 13.
47. "On Meeting Authors."
48. "On Meeting Authors."
49. Malcolm Cowley, "How Writers Earn Their Livings," *Saturday Review of Literature*, September 25, 1954, 9.
50. "How Writers Earn Their Livings."
51. "Toward an American Language," *Atlantic*, 1952.
52. Van Wyck Brooks, *The Writer in America* (New York: E.P. Dutton, 1953) 63.
53. "How Writers Live," *Time*, January 10, 1955, 86.

54. "How Writers Live."
55. "How Writers Live."
56. Benedict Thielen, "Advice to a Girl About to Marry a Writer," *Harper's Magazine*, September 1955, 85.
57. "Slick Sociology," *Nation*, 1957.
58. Raymond Walters, Jr., "Intellectuals in Gray Flannel Suits," *The Saturday Review*, September 14, 1957, 28.
59. "The Disorganization Man," *Time*, June 9, 1958, 100.
60. "The Disorganization Man."
61. Granville Hicks, "The Quest in a Quiet Time," *The Saturday Review*, November 28, 1959, 20.
62. Larston D. Farrar, "The Challenges Facing Writers," *Vital Speeches of the Day*, December 15, 1959, 150.

Chapter 3

1. Norman Cousins, "Editorial: When American and Soviet Writers Meet," *Saturday Review*, June 24, 1978, 42; A group of nine American writers including James Baldwin and Toni Morrison met with Soviet counterparts at the Black Sea resort of Pitsunda the following year.
2. Curtis G. Benjamin, "The Industry That Disdains Success," *Saturday Review*, June 25, 1960, 13.
3. Granville Hicks, "The Writer's New Peril—Status," "The Industry That Disdains Success," *Saturday Review*, June 25, 1960, 18.
4. Dr. Robert L. Oliver, "Writers Are People," *Vital Speeches of the Day*, July 1, 1961, 571.
5. Paul R. Reynolds, "So You Want to Write a Book," *Saturday Review*, July 13, 1963, 48.
6. "Writers Are People."
7. "Writers Are People."
8. Granville Hicks, "These Are Their Lives," *Saturday Review*, November 4, 1961, 21.
9. "So You Want to Write a Book."
10. Edward T. Ewen, "Poet, Actor, Painter—Cabbie," *New York Times Magazine*, October 27, 1963, 217.
11. Alan Pryce-Jones, "How to Act Like a Writer in New York and London," *Saturday Review*, November 1965, 146.
12. Richard Schickel, "The Big Money Writers," *Life*, July 31, 1964, 58.
13. "The Big Money Writers."
14. William Saroyan, "It's Me, O Lord!," *Saturday Evening Post*, April 18, 1964, 75–76.
15. Robert J. Clements, "Is the Nobel Prize for Literature Political?," *Saturday Review*, December 4, 1965, 41.
16. Irving Howe, "The Writer Can't Keep to His Attic," *New York Times Magazine*, December 5, 1965, SM43.
17. John W. Finney, "24 Writers Urge New Steps for Vietnam Peace," *New York Times*, April 27, 1966, 6.
18. "220 Writers Urge Continuing of War," *New York Times*, December 24, 1968, 14.
19. "Granville Hicks, "Sagas of the Underprivileged," *Saturday Review*, August 28, 1965, 29.
20. Harvey Swados, "The Coming Revolution in Literature," *Saturday Review*, August 21, 1965, 14.
21. "The Coming Revolution in Literature."
22. Henry Raymont, "U.S. Writers Ask Soviet to Free 2," *New York Times*, January 22, 1968, 13.
23. "Group Formed in U.S. to Protest Soviet Treatment of Solzhenitsyn," *New York Times*, August 29, 1972, 2.
24. "Writers Appeal on Soviet Jews," *New York Times*, May 21, 1967, 12.
25. Henry Raymont, "Writers Appeal for Soviet Jews," *New York Times*, August 3, 1969, 6.
26. "33 Here Criticize Poland on Jews," *New York Times*, January 24, 1969, 7.
27. Herbert Mitgang, "U.S. Writers Seeking Support for Czech Dissidents," *New York Times*, January 23, 1977, 8.
28. "Lance for Hire," *Time*, September 15, 1967, 82.

29. "Lance for Hire."
30. "Lance for Hire."
31. "Lance for Hire."
32. Rex Lardner, "Agony in the Attic," *Saturday Review*, January 9, 1971, 47.
33. "Agony in the Attic."
34. "Agony in the Attic."
35. "Agony in the Attic."
36. "Grub Street Revisited," *Time*, April 10, 1978, 75.
37. John Tebbel, "When a Book Hits the Jackpot," *Saturday Review*, February 12, 1966, 62.
38. Granville Hicks, "To Him Who Would a Writer Be," *Saturday Review*, January 1, 1966, 23.
39. Cathey and Edward Pinckney, "Can I Have One?," *Saturday Review*, February 12, 1966, 61.
40. "Can I Have One?"
41. Granville Hicks, "Obsolete at Thirty," *Saturday Review*, December 2, 1967, 25.
42. John Leonard, "Books of the Times," *New York Times*, October 23, 1970, 38.
43. Robert Brustein, "If an Artist Wants To Be Serious and Respected and Rich, Famous and Popular, He Is Suffering From Cultural Schizophrenia," *New York Times Magazine*, September 26, 1971, SM12.
44. "If an Artist Wants To Be Serious and Respected and Rich, Famous and Popular, He Is Suffering From Cultural Schizophrenia."
45. Thomas Meehan, "The Yale Faculty Makes the Scene," *New York Times Magazine*, February 7, 1971, SM12.
46. "The Celebrity Monger," *The Nation*, November 12, 1977, 486.
47. Robert Brustein, "If an Artist Wants To Be Serious and Respected and Rich, Famous and Popular, He Is Suffering From Cultural Schizophrenia," *New York Times Magazine*, September 26, 1971, SM12.
48. "The Novel: Very Warm for May," *Time*, May 7, 1973, 71.
49. Ted Solotaroff, "Cult of Masculinity in American Fiction," *Esquire*, October 1972, 82.
50. "The Masculine Wilderness of the American Novel," *Saturday Review*, January 29, 1972, 41–44.
51. Anatole Broyard, "An Age of Untidy Tragedy," *New York Times*, January 24, 1974, 35.
52. Aristides, "A Literary Mafia?," *American Scholar*, Spring 1975, 182.
53. "A Literary Mafia?"
54. Alfred Kazin, "'The Giant Killer': Drink & the American Writer," *Commentary*, March 1976, 44.
55. "'The Giant Killer': Drink & the American Writer."
56. "The Writer's Vice," *Time*, October 5, 1970, 73.
57. Mark Harris, "The Perils of the Novelist," *New York Times*, January 4, 1976, BR7.
58. Walter Beacham, "Against the Grain," *The Nation*, June 11, 1977, 729.
59. James A. Michener, "Author James Michener on Future of this Country," *U.S. News & World Report*, September 12, 1977, 60.
60. Lewis H. Lapham, "The Cave of the Winds," *National Review*, September 16, 1977, 1055–1060.
61. Jason Berry, "The Search for Roots," *The Nation*, October 2, 1976, 313–315.
62. James A. Michener, "'Roots,' Unique in Its Time," *New York Times*, February 27, 1977, 241.
63. "'Roots,' Unique in Its Time."
64. Herbert Mitgang, "Behind the Best Sellers," *New York Times*, January 29, 1978, BR10.
65. E.J. Kahn Jr., "Literary Life on the Cape," *New York Times Book Review*, June 4, 1978, BR4.
66. Nora Sayre, "at MacDowell and Yaddo," *New York Times Book Review*, June 4, 1978, BR4.
67. John Knowles, "...In the Hamptons...," *New York Times Book Review*, June 4, 1978, BR4.

Chapter 4

1. Ian Hamilton, "Killjoy," *New York Times*, June 8, 1997, SM74.
2. Anita Shreve, "The American Short Story: An Untold Tale," *New York Times*, November 30, 1980, SM34.
3. Ronald Sukenick, "Up From the Garret: Success Then and Now," *New York Times*, January 27, 1985, BR1.
4. David Quammen, "A Cheap Hide-Out for Writers," *New York Times*, November 1, 1981, BR4.
5. Herbert Gold, "The Loneliness of the Long-Distance Writer," *New York Times*, February 13, 1983, BR11.
6. Jane O'Reilly, "In Key West: The Writer as a Star," *Time*, February 6, 1984, 13.
7. "Brooklyn, Borough of Writers," *New York Times*, May 8, 1983, BR12.
8. Michiko Kautani, "As the Author Grows Up," *New York Times*, July 25, 1982, BR27.
9. Helen Benedict, "A Writer's First Readers," *New York Times*, February 6, 1983, BR11.
10. Michiko Kakutani, "Dashers and Dawdlers," *New York Times*, August 21, 1983, BR31.
11. Thomas Fleming, "The War Between Writers and Reviewers," *New York Times*, January 6, 1985, BR3.
12. Thomas Fleming, "The War Between Writers and Reviewers."
13. Joyce Carol Oates, "The World's Worst Critics," *New York Times*, January 18, 1987, BR1.
14. Charles Salzberg, "Postwritum Depression, False Stagnancy and Other Ills Caused by Writing Books," *New York Times*, March 8, 1987, BR372.
15. "Postwritum Depression, False Stagnancy and Other Ills Caused by Writing Books."
16. Lawrence Shainberg, "Full of Hope? We Can Cure That," *New York Times*, September 11, 1988, BR1.
17. Bonita Friedman, "Envy, the Writer's Disease," *New York Times*, November 26, 1989, BR1.
18. Anatole Broyard, "Writers Beware Writers," *New York Times*, May 21, 1989, BR14.
19. Linda Bamber, "Writers Can Be Friends," *New York Times*, December 14, 1986, BR1.
20. Joshua Hammer, "Not Such a Happy Ending," *Newsweek*, January 15, 1990, 48.
21. William F. Buckley Jr., "Hawking Your Books," *National Review*, November 4, 1991, 63.
22. "Hawking Your Books."
23. Sven Birkets, "Mapping the New Reality," *Wilson Quarterly*, Spring 1992, 102.
24. "Mapping the New Reality."
25. Nicolas Lemann, "Missed Moorings—American Novelists Lose Touch," *Washington Monthly*, February 1986, 43.
26. Jeffrey Giles, "The Selling of the Young," *National Review*, November 20, 1987, 64.
27. Lisa See Kendall, "Works by Native American Writers Find Wider Audience," *Publishers Weekly*, September 28, 1990, 80.
28. Joseph Barbato, "Latino Writers in the American Market," *Publishers Weekly*, February 1, 1991, 17.
29. "The Big Aiiieeeee!: An Anthology of Chinese American and Japanese American Literature," *Publishers Weekly*, May 31, 1991, 67.
30. Joseph Barbato, "'Black an Read' at ABA," *Publishers Weekly*, May 11, 1990, 225.
31. Calvin Reid, "Building a Readership," *Publishers Weekly*, January 20, 1992, 36.
32. Paul Nathan and Calvin Reid, "Pocket Books Gets 'Exhale' for Near Record $2.6M," *Publishers Weekly*, July 13, 1992, 9.
33. "Black Schools Urged to Offer Campus Writing Degree Programs," *Jet*, August 30, 1993, 22.
34. Maureen O'Brien, "Novelist Toni

Morrison Wins Nobel Prize for Literature," *Publishers Weekly*, October 11, 1993, 7.

35. "Morrison's Books are Hot Properties in Hollywood," *Jet*, November 15, 1993, 58.

36. "The Year of the Black Author," *Black Enterprise*, February 1995, 116.

37. Carolyn M. Brown, "Writing a New Chapter in Book Publishing," *Black Enterprise*, February 1995, 108.

38. Michael Cart, "Invisible No Longer," *Booklist*, February 15, 1995, 1069.

39. Elizabeth Yates, "Facing Up to Time," *Writer*, March 1998, 5.

40. Judith Alguire, "Ah, Solitude!," *Writer*, May 1993, 7.

41. D.M. Murray, "A Writer's Habits," *Writer*, January 1992, 14.

42. Nancy Springer, "Lonesome Hills, Purple Sky," *Writer*, June 1993, 7.

43. "Ah, Solitude!"

44. Arthur Krystal, "The Writing Life," *American Scholar*, Spring 1997, 286.

45. Portia Steele, "Beyond the Keyboard," *Writer*, December 1993, 7.

46. Robert Reilly, "Writing as Contemplation," *America*, September 18, 1999, 6.

47. Colleen Mariah Rae, "The Creative Power of Doing Nothing," *Writer*, July 1997, 13.

48. Aristides, "Compose Yourself," *American Scholar*, Fall 1992, 487.

49. Jeffrey Skinner and Stephen Phillip Policoff, "Writer's Block—and What to Do About It," *Writer*, November 1994, 21.

50. Fran Lebowitz, "On Not Writing," *Harper's Magazine*, November 1993, 34.

51. Diane Lefer, "Writer—Or Fraud?," *Writer*, June 1995, 5.

52. Genie Dickerson, "Keep Your Writing on Track," *Writer*, August 1998, 25.

53. Margaret Chittenden, "Perspiration and Inspiration," *Writer*, May 1995, 13.

54. J.A. McConney, "The Writer and the Noonday Devil," *Writer*, January 1993, 7.

55. Peggy Rynk, "Waiting for Inspiration," *Writer*, September 1992, 9.

56. "Compose Yourself."

57. Maia Wojciechowska, "Building Self-Confidence," *Writer*, May 1996, 5.

58. Warren Kiefer, "What Makes a Writer Tick?," *Writer*, June 1993, 9.

59. Kelley Cherry, "Beginning," *Writer*, November 1995, 22.

60. Melannie Svoboda, "The Eight Beatitudes of Writing," *America*, November 11, 1995, 24.

61. Jane Yolen, "Writing With Joy," *Writer*, February 1999, 6.

62. Erica Jong, "Doing It for Love," *Writer*, July 1997, 3.

63. James Atlas, "The Age of the Literary Memoir is Now," *New York Times*, May 12, 1996, SM25.

64. Mordecai Richler, "The Write Stuff," *Saturday Night*, February 1997, 41.

65. Trudi M. Rosenblum, "Authors on Audio," *Publishers Weekly*, June 1, 1998, S4.

66. "Authors on Audio."

67. Sara Paretsky, "Damned by Dollars," *American Scholar*, Winter 1999, 160; Paretsky had borrowed the phrase from Herman Melville who, in describing his poverty in a letter to Nathaniel Hawthorne, stated that "dollars damn me."

68. Matthew Klam, "Some of My Best Friends are Rich," *New York Times*, June 7, 1998, SM64.

69. Adam Hochschild, "On the Road Again," *New York Times*, October 17, 1999, BR394.

Chapter 5

1. Lynne Sharon Schwartz, "Clicking the Habit," *New York Times Magazine*, June 4, 2000, SM6).

2. Stephen King, "My Screen Addiction," *Entertainment Weekly*, July 31, 2009, 20.

Chapter Notes—5

3. Mark Jacobson, "The Laptop Nomads," *New York*, May 15, 2000, 28.
4. Joan Mazza, "How I Killed My Novel," *Writer*, October 2000, 5.
5. Sherwin B. Nuland, "The Uncertain Art," *The American Scholar*, Winter 2001, 130.
6. Eileen Herbert Jordan, "Wooing the Muse," *Writer*, June 2000, 5.
7. Jana Carvajal, "The Writer Within You," *Writer*, September 2000, 6.
8. Dan Brown, "A Time to Thrill," *O, The Oprah Magazine*, September 2003, 206.
9. Mark Fitzgerald, "Position Wanted," *Writer*, July 2003, 26.
10. "Day Jobs," *Lapham's Quarterly*, Spring 2010, 62.
11. Justin Kramon, "Day Jobs That Help you Get Your Writing Done," *Writer*, August 2011, 32–35.
12. "Position Wanted."
13. Sandra Hurtes, "Writing on the Fly," *Writer*, December 2008, 30–55.
14. Michael Ledwidge, "Thinking Like a Criminal," *Writer*, July 2003, 30.
15. Michelle Silver, "Isolation Blues," *Writer*, August 2003, 19.
16. Rebecca Troyer Robbins, "That Irresistible Urge," *Writer*, September 2003, 30.
17. Marilyn Ross, Cal Orey, and Magdalena Ball, "An Expert's Guide to Successful Self-Publishing," *Writer*, February 2004, 31–38.
18. Joshua Davidovich, "One for the Blooks," *U.S. News & World Report*, March 13, 2006, 52–53.
19. Michael Kinsley, "Writers Rule!," *Time*, April 21, 2008, 78.
20. Nancy Hendrickson, "Use Podcasts to Promote Your Book," *Writer*, November 2007, 36.
21. Scott Sigler, "Writer Podcasts His Way to a 3-Book Contract," *Writer*, October 2008, 14.
22. Steve Saffel, "Consider a Multiplatform Approach," *Writer*, August 2009, 40–41.
23. David Skinner, "Books 'R' Us," *The Weekly Standard*, October 10, 2005, 48.
24. Curtis Sittenfeld, "You Can't Get a Man With a Pen," *New York Times*, December 19, 2004, BR35.
25. Elizabeth Royte, "Publish and Perish," *New York Times*, October 23, 2005, F31.
26. David Amsden,"Fly Like an Ego," *New York*, August 29–September 5, 2005, 166.
27. Sarah Anne Johnson, "What's a Memoir Writer To Do?," *Writer*, November 2006, 20–23.
28. Geoff Nicholson, "Can't. Stop. Writing." *New York Times*, February 22, 2009, A23.
29. Lisa Shearin, "Dealing With a 3:30 A.M. Wake-Up Call from the Muse," *Writer*, August 2010, 10.
30. "Dealing With a 3:30 A.M. Wake-Up Call from the Muse."
31. Michael Meyer, "About That Advance...," *New York Times*, April 12, 2009, A27.
32. "About That Advance..."
33. Arthur Krystal, "When Writers Speak," *New York Times*, September 27, 2009, A27.
34. Rachel Donadio, "More Bang for the Book," *New York Times*, July 27, 2008, C27.
35. Paul Greenberg, "Bail Out the Writers," *New York Times*, December 14, 2008, B27.
36. "Bail Out the Writers."
37. Joe Queenan, "Over the Transom," *The Weekly Standard*, August 9, 2010, 37–38.
38. "A Tale of Two Literary Cultures," *Wilson Quarterly*, Spring 2011, 79.
39. Dan Kois, "Burn Before Reading," *New York Times Book Review*, March 6, 2011, BR27.
40. Joseph Epstein, "Finito, I Guess," *The Weekly Standard*, October 18, 2010, 5.
41. "Finito, I Guess."
42. Isia Jasiewicz, "Who Needs a Publisher?," *Newsweek*, August 9, 2010, 47.

Chapter Notes—5

43. Jennie Yabroff, "The Man We Knew Too Much," *Newsweek*, September 6, 2010, 50.

44. Leon Wieseltier, "The New Proles," *The New Republic*, February 4, 2010, 40.

45. Susan Johnston, "Blogging for Bucks," *Writer*, August 2011, 47–47.

46. Joseph Finora, "Going Beyond Books and Magazines," *The Writer*, October 2012, 40–41.

47. Susan Cheever, "Please Stop Writing!," *Newsweek*, March 28, 2011, 74–75.

48. Gail Godwin, "Working On the Ending," *New York Times Book Review*, December 12, 2010, A31.

49. Stephen Marche, "A Thousand Words," *Esquire*, December 2012, 90.

50. "A Thousand Words."

51. Natalie Robehmed, "The World's Top-Earning Authors," *Forbes*, August 17, 2015, 1.

52. Rachel Deahl, "The Rise of the Seven-Figure Advance," *Publishers Weekly*, November 24, 2014, 1.

53. Calvin Wilson, "Washington U. Grad Writes One of Year's Hottest Novels," *St. Louis Post-Dispatch*, October 17, 2015, accessed online; Stuart Emmrich, "The Literary Wunderkind of the Year," *New York Times*, December 20, 2015, 20(L).

54. Alexandra Alter, "Fans Online and, Perhaps, at Bookstores," *New York Times*, May 6, 2015.

55. Neal Gabler, "The Secret Shame of Middle-Class Americans," *The Atlantic.com*, May 2016, accessed online.

56. Matt A.V. Chaban, "A Literary House Keeps the Spirit of Greenwich Village Alive," *New York Times*, March 29, 2016, A23(L).

57. Jennifer Schuessler, "Nice Chicago Address for a Writers Museum," *New York Times*, October 25, 2015, C3(L); Matt Beardmore, "Author, Author," *New York Times*, December 27, 2015, 3(L).

58. Robert Gottlieb, *Avid Reader: A Life* (New York: Farrar, Straus and Giroux, 2016).

59. "'America Reads' Exhibition to Open June 16," *State News Service*, May 26, 2016.

60. "Chipotle Launches New Installment of 'Cultivating Thought' Author Series on Cups and Bags," *Business Wire*, January 27, 2015, accessed online.

Bibliography

Baym, Nina, ed. *The Norton Anthology of American Literature*. New York: W.W. Norton & Company, 2007.

Bercovitch, Sacvan. *The American Jeremiad*. Madison: University of Wisconsin Press, 1978.

Bloom, Harold. *The Daemon Knows: Literary Greatness and the American Sublime*. New York: Spiegel & Grau, 2015.

Brooks, Van Wyck. *The Writer in America*. New York: E.P. Dutton, 1953.

Goodwin, Donald W., M.D. *Alcohol and the Writer*. New York: Penguin, 1990.

Gottlieb, Robert. *Avid Reader: A Life*. New York: Farrar, Straus and Giroux, 2016.

Gray, Richard. *A History of American Literature*. Hoboken, NJ: Blackwell, 2004.

Kazin, Alfred. *God and the American Writer*. New York: Knopf, 1997.

Kimball, George and John Schulian, eds. *At the Fights: American Writers on Boxing*. New York: Library of America, 2012.

Kostelanetz, Richard, ed. *The Young American Writers*. New York: Funk & Wagnalls, 1967.

Laing, Olivia. *The Trip to Echo Spring: On Writers and Drinking*. New York: Picador, 2014.

Marcus, Greil and Werner Sollors, eds. *A New Literary History of America*. Cambridge, MA: Belknap Press, 2009.

Mendeson, Edward. *Moral Agents: Eight Twentieth-Century American Writers*. New York: New York Review Books, 2015.

Tarnoff, Ben. *The Bohemians: Mark Twain and the San Francisco Writers Who Reinvented American Literature*. New York: Penguin, 2014.

Van Doren, Carl. *Contemporary American Novelists, 1900–1920*. New York: Macmillan, 1922.

Index

Academy Award 72
Adaptation 9
African Americans 19, 89–90, 105–107
Albee, Edward 65, 76, 92
alcohol (drinking) 9, 86–87
Alcott, Louisa May 141
Algonquin Round Table ("Vicious Circle") 12, 17
Allen, Woody 16, 108
Amazon 128, 130, 131, 138
American Splendor 9
Anderson, Maxwell 28
Anderson, Sherwood 12, 17, 20, 22, 28, 29, 50
Angelou, Maya 106
Arendt, Hannah 75
Asian Americans 105
Atherton, Gertrude 14
Auchincloss, Louis 55
audiobooks 117–118

Baldwin, James 74
Baretta 88
Barnes, Margaret Ayer 36
Barth, John 82
Barton Fink 2
The Beats 10, 18, 61, 62–63, 94
Bell, Daniel 75
Bellow, Saul 9, 58, 63, 67, 73, 75, 81, 88, 131, 137
Beloved 106
Benchley, Robert 40
Berryman, John 9, 86
blogs 128, 130, 138, 139–140, 142, 143
book clubs 45, 46, 49, 59, 119
Boothe, Claire 38
Brallier, Max 144

Bromfield, Louis 36
Brooks, Van Wyck 58
Brown, Dan 123–124
Buchwald, Art 91
Buck, Pearl 12, 41, 73
Buckley, William F., Jr. 74, 75
Burrough, Bryan 4
Burroughs, Augusten 132, 146

Cabell, James Branch 19
Caldwell, Erskine 85, 88
Californication 9
Capote 9
Capote, Truman 8, 10, 49, 81, 85, 92, 137
Carter, Jimmy 76, 117
Cartland, Barbara 132
Carver, Raymond 9
Cather, Willa 22, 30, 35, 50, 55, 111
Cerf, Bennett 38
Chabon, Michael 137, 142
Chandler, Raymond 10
Charyn, Jerome 82
Cheever, John 9, 84, 91
Cheever, Susan 141
Civil War 16, 17, 29, 41, 80
Cold War 50, 62, 64, 65
Conrad, Joseph 21, 125
Cosby, Bill 102
counterculture 63, 74, 75, 93, 95
Coward, Noel 40
Crane, Hart 86, 96
Cummings, E.E. 21, 49, 86

The Da Vinci Code 124
Davis, H.L. 36
Deathtrap 9
Deconstructing Harry 9

161

Index

DeLillo, Don 144
De Vries, Peter 58, 84
Diaz, Junot 137, 142, 145
Didion, Joan 88, 97
Dos Passos, John 12, 14, 20, 30, 35, 48, 49, 74, 85, 96
Dreiser, Theodore 11, 17, 20, 22, 30, 35, 50
Dunne, John Gregory 97

e-books 138, 142
Egan, Jennifer 137
Eggers, Dave 134
Ellis, Bret Easton 104, 131
Ellison, Ralph 55, 58, 67, 75, 76, 107
Emerson, Ralph Waldo 10, 22, 135, 145
Ephron, Nora 146
Erskine, John 44–45

Farrar, Larston D. 63
Faulkner, William 9, 12, 19, 48, 49, 52, 69, 73, 83, 86, 88, 104, 124
Fear and Loathing in Las Vegas 9
Federal Writer's Project 135–136
Ferber, Edna 32, 38, 40, 50
Finding Forrester 9
Fitzgerald, F. Scott 9, 12, 13–14, 21, 30, 35, 49, 54, 55, 83, 86–87, 143
Foer, Jonathan Safran 130, 138, 145, 146
Franzen, Jonathan 138–139, 144
Frey, James 131–132
The Front Page 39
Frost, Robert 8, 19, 96

Gabler, Neal 145
Gale, Zona 22
Ginsberg, Allen 62, 76
Glasgow, Ellen 35, 88
Gone with the Wind 34–35, 41
Goodwin, Doris Kearns 135
Gotham Writers 6
Grafton, Sue 123
Graham, Katherine 146
Gray, John 117
Great American Novel 10, 56, 60, 66, 84, 142, 143, 144
Great Depression 5, 12, 23, 33–34, 36, 50, 61
Green, John 143

Grey, Zane 58
Gunga Din 39

Haley, Alex 89–90
Hallberg, Garth Risk 144, 145
Hammett, Dashiell 86
Harburg, Yip 75
Harris, E. Lynn 107
Harris, Mark 67, 87
Hart, Moss 38
Hecht, Ben 17, 22, 39
Heller, Joseph 58, 74, 92, 141, 146
Hellman, Lillian 8, 38, 91
Hemingway, Ernest 9, 12, 21, 22, 35, 38, 48, 49, 52, 54, 73, 85, 86, 87, 95, 111, 143
Henry, O. 58
Hergesheimer, Joseph 14
Herrick, Robert 20–21
Hersey, John 53, 76
Heyward, Edwin DuBose 19
Hijuelos, Oscar 105
Hispanic Americans 105
Hochschild, Adam 119
Hollywood 34–35, 36, 39, 41, 44, 47, 48, 49, 56, 71, 83
Holmes, Clellon 62
Howe, Irving 73, 75
The Human Comedy 72

Irving, John 8, 144
Isaacson, Walter 146

James, Henry 55
Jones, James 38, 82, 84
Jones, LeRoi 82
Jong, Erica 116

Karr, Mary 116
Kaysen, Susanna 116
Kazin, Alfred 6, 67, 73, 86, 87
Kelland, Clarence Budington 31
Kelly, William Melvin 82
Kerouac, Jack 62
King, Stephen 118, 120, 137
Kingsolver, Barbara 146
Kinney, Jeff 144
Kinsley, Michael 128–129
Knopf, Alfred 91
Kojak 88
Koontz, Dean 132

Index

LaFarge, Oliver 36
Laing, Olivia 9
Lapham, Lewis H. 88–89
Lardner, Ring 86
Lebowitz, Fran 111
Lee, Harper 58, 137, 141
Lerner, Max 37
Lessing, Doris 84
Lethem, Jonathan 145
Lewis, Sinclair 12, 13, 14, 20, 22, 35, 39, 50, 73, 86
literary agents 24, 25, 30, 40, 68, 71, 80, 96, 98, 102, 104, 107, 114, 121, 128, 129, 134, 136, 138, 139
literary societies 26, 45
London, Jack 86
Longfellow, Henry Wadsworth 12
Love Story 83
Lowell, James Russell 12
Lowell, Robert 73
Luce, Henry 38
Lulu Blooker Prize 128
Lynd, Helen 21
Lynd, Robert 21

MacLeish, Archibald 50, 75
Mailer, Norman 8, 49, 58, 63, 69, 82, 84, 141
Malamud, Bernard 84, 88
Manhattan 9
Marche, Stephen 120, 142–143, 145
Marquand, J.P. (John) 40, 48, 86
Masson, Thomas L. 11
McCall, Nathan 107
McCarthy, Mary 8, 67, 81
McCullers, Carson 9, 63
McInerney, Jay 104
McMillan, Terry 106
Melville, Herman 59
Mencken, H.L. 17, 19
Michener, James 71, 88, 90
Midnight in Paris 16
Millay, Edna St. Vincent 9, 86
Miller, Arthur 65, 73, 75, 76, 83
Miller, Caroline 36
Miller, Heather Ross 82
Miller, Henry 12
Mitchell, Margaret 34, 35
Morley, Christopher 40

Morris, Wright 63
Morrison, Toni 106
Mosley, Walter 107
Moulitsas, Markos 128
movies: 126, 130, 143; *Adaptation* 9; *American Splendor* 9; *Barton Fink* 2; *Beloved* 106; *Capote* 9; *The Da Vinci Code* 124; *Deathtrap* 9; *Deconstructing Harry* 9; *Fear and Loathing in Las Vegas* 9; *Finding Forrester* 9; *The Front Page* 39; *Gone with the Wind* 34–35, 41; *Gunga Din* 39; *The Human Comedy* 72; *Love Story* 83; *Manhattan* 9; *Midnight in Paris* 16; *Our Town* 40; *The Player* 9; *The Royal Tenenbaums* 9; *Scarface* 39; *The Shining* 9; *Sideways* 9; *The Squid and the Whale* 9; *Sunset Blvd.* 2; *The Third Man* 31; *The Wizard of Oz* 75; *Wonder Boys* 9; *The World According to Garp* 9; *Wuthering Heights* 39
Murder She Wrote 9
Murdoch, Iris 84

Nathan, George Jean 30
National Book Award 55, 88, 142–143
National Medal of Arts 55
Native Americans 105
Nobel Prize in Literature 41, 42, 72, 75, 86, 106
Norris, Frank 17
Nuland, Sherwin B. 122

Oates, Joyce Carol 65, 82, 88, 99, 132, 145
O'Brien, Edna 146
O'Connor, Flannery 63
Odets, Clifford 83
O'Hara, John 48, 52–53
O'Neill, Eugene 12, 73, 86, 91
Oprah 132
Our Town 40

Paretsky, Sara 118
Parker, Dorothy 38, 86
Parsons, Louella 38
Patterson, James 132, 143
Plath, Sylvia 58
The Player 9
Plimpton, George 92

Index

podcasts 129
Poe, Edgar Allan 22, 58, 86
Porter, Katherine Anne 48, 59, 81
Priestley, J.B. 25
prizes 101
psychoanalysis 20, 22, 27, 53, 57, 60, 122
Pulitzer Prize 35–36, 40, 41, 42, 72, 75, 87–88, 106, 125, 143

Queenan, Joe 136

Rice, Anne 118
Rice, Elmer 53–54
Rich, Louise Dickenson 46
Rich Man, Poor Man 90
Roach, Mary 131
Robbins, Harold 71, 90–91
Roots 89–90
Roth, Philip 9, 58, 82, 84, 131, 141
Roth, Veronica 143
The Royal Tenenbaums 9
Runyon, Damon 38, 48

Salinger, J.D. 58, 63, 69
Sandburg, Carl 17, 50
Saroyan, William 38, 49, 72
Scarface 39
Schlesinger, Arthur 75, 76
Segal, Erich 83
Shaw, Irwin 90
Sherwood, Robert 28
The Shining 9
Sideways 9
Sinclair, Upton 88
social media 131
Solzhenitsyn, Aleksandr 75
Sontag, Susan 82, 84
The Squid and the Whale 9
Steel, Danielle 132
Stegner, Wallace 59
Steinbeck, John 12, 35, 48, 73, 85, 86, 91
Stevens, Wallace 8, 86, 125
Stowe, Harriet Beecher 145
Stribling, T.S. 36
Styron, William 76, 89, 116
Sunset Blvd. 2

Tabori, Paul 47–48
Tan, Amy 105, 146
Tarkington, Booth 17, 19, 29, 35

television 130; *Baretta* 88; *Californication* 9; *Kojak* 88; *Murder She Wrote* 9; *Oprah* 132; *Rich Man, Poor Man* 90; *Roots* 89–90; *The Today Show* 131; *The Tonight Show* 83
The Third Man 31
Thoreau, Henry David 22
Thurber, James 58
The Today Show 131
The Tonight Show 83
Towne, Charles Hanson 40
Trilling, Lionel 59
Twain, Mark 5, 22, 135
Turow, Scott 106

Updike, John 8, 9, 58, 65, 82, 92, 132, 137
Uris, Leon 90

Van Doren, Carl 13–14
Vidal, Gore 8, 49, 82
videogames 130, 142
Vietnam War 73, 74
Vonnegut, Kurt 9, 65, 76, 84, 115

Wallace, David Foster 130, 131
Wallace, Irving 71, 90
Warren, Robert Penn 48, 75
West, Cornell 107
Wharton, Edith 19, 30, 35, 55
Whitman, Walt 16, 22, 96, 131–132, 145
Wilder, Thornton 32, 40
Williams, Tennessee 9, 49, 54, 96
Wilson, Edmund 91
Wilson, Margaret 36
Winchell, Walter 38
Winfrey, Oprah 106, 116, 119, 130, 132
The Wizard of Oz 75
Wolfe, Thomas 50
Wolfe, Tom 8, 104, 131, 142, 144
Wonder Boys 9
Woollcott, Alexander 38, 39
The World According to Garp 9
World War I 4, 11, 12, 21, 30, 34, 44, 48, 61
World War II 5, 11, 12, 21, 30, 38, 43–44, 46–50, 54, 61, 72, 84
Wouk, Herman 38, 71
Wuthering Heights 39

www.ingramcontent.com/pod-product-compliance
Ingram Content Group UK Ltd.
Pitfield, Milton Keynes, MK11 3LW, UK
UKHW042016140426
5217IPUK00015B/1208